Balancing and Weighing

TEACHER'S GUIDE

SCIENCE AND TECHNOLOGY FOR CHILDREN

NATIONAL SCIENCE RESOURCES CENTER
Smithsonian Institution • National Academy of Sciences
Arts and Industries Building, Room 1201
Washington, DC 20560

NSRC

The National Science Resources Center is operated by the Smithsonian Institution and the National Academy of Sciences to improve the teaching of science in the nation's schools. The NSRC collects and disseminates information about exemplary teaching resources, develops and disseminates curriculum materials, and sponsors outreach activities, specifically in the areas of leadership development and technical assistance, to help school districts develop and sustain hands-on science programs.

STC Project Supporters

National Science Foundation
Smithsonian Institution
U.S. Department of Defense
U.S. Department of Education
John D. and Catherine T. MacArthur Foundation
The Dow Chemical Company Foundation
E. I. du Pont de Nemours & Company
Amoco Foundation, Inc.
Hewlett-Packard Company
Smithsonian Institution Educational Outreach Fund

This project was supported, in part,
by the
National Science Foundation
Opinions expressed are those of the authors
and not necessarily those of the Foundation

ISBN 0-89278-729-5

Published by Carolina Biological Supply Company, 2700 York Road, Burlington, NC 27215.
Call toll free 1-800-334-5551.

This material is based upon work supported by the National Science Foundation under Grant No. ESI-9252947. Any opinions, findings, and conclusions or recommendations expressed in this material are those of the author(s) and do not necessarily reflect the views of the National Science Foundation.

CB787269803
♲ Printed on recycled paper.

Foreword

Since 1988, the National Science Resources Center (NSRC) has been developing Science and Technology for Children (STC), an innovative hands-on science program for children in grades one through six. The 24 units of the STC program, four for each grade level, are designed to provide all students with stimulating experiences in the life, earth, and physical sciences and technology while simultaneously developing their critical-thinking and problem-solving skills.

Sequence of STC Units

Grade	Life, Earth, and Physical Sciences and Technology			
1	Organisms	Weather	Solids and Liquids	Comparing and Measuring
2	The Life Cycle of Butterflies	Soils	Changes	Balancing and Weighing
3	Plant Growth and Development	Rocks and Minerals	Chemical Tests	Sound
4	Animal Studies	Land and Water	Electric Circuits	Motion and Design
5	Microworlds	Ecosystems	Food Chemistry	Floating and Sinking
6	Experiments with Plants	Measuring Time	Magnets and Motors	The Technology of Paper

The STC units provide children with the opportunity to learn age-appropriate concepts and skills and to acquire scientific attitudes and habits of mind. In the primary grades, children begin their study of science by observing, measuring, and identifying properties. Then they move on through a progression of experiences that culminate in grade six with the design of controlled experiments.

Sequence of Development of Scientific Reasoning Skills

Scientific Reasoning Skills	Grades					
	1	2	3	4	5	6
Observing, Measuring, and Identifying Properties	♦	♦	♦	♦	♦	♦
Seeking Evidence Recognizing Patterns and Cycles		♦	♦	♦	♦	♦
Identifying Cause and Effect Extending the Senses				♦	♦	♦
Designing and Conducting Controlled Experiments						♦

The "Focus-Explore-Reflect-Apply" learning cycle incorporated into the STC units is based on research findings about children's learning. These findings indicate that knowledge is actively constructed by each learner and that children learn science best in a hands-on experimental environment where they can make their own discoveries. The steps of the learning cycle are as follows:

- Focus: Explore and clarify the ideas that children already have about the topic.

- Explore: Enable children to engage in hands-on explorations of the objects, organisms, and science phenomena to be investigated.

- Reflect: Encourage children to discuss their observations and to reconcile their ideas.

- Apply: Help children discuss and apply their new ideas in new situations.

The learning cycle in STC units gives students opportunities to develop increased understanding of important scientific concepts and to develop positive attitudes toward science.

The STC units provide teachers with a variety of strategies with which to assess student learning. The STC units also offer teachers opportunities to link the teaching of science with the development of skills in mathematics, language arts, and social studies. In addition, the STC units encourage the use of cooperative learning to help students develop the valuable skill of working together.

In the extensive research and development process used with all STC units, scientists and educators, including experienced elementary school teachers, act as consultants to teacher-developers, who research, trial teach, and write the units. The process begins with the developer researching the unit's content and pedagogy. Then, before writing the unit, the developer trial teaches lessons in public school classrooms in the metropolitan Washington, D.C., area. Once a unit is written, the NSRC evaluates its effectiveness with children by field-testing it nationally in ethnically diverse urban, rural, and suburban public schools. At the field-testing stage, the assessment sections in each unit are also evaluated by the Program Evaluation and Research Group of Lesley College, located in Cambridge, Mass. The final editions of the units reflect the incorporation of teacher and student field-test feedback and of comments on accuracy and soundness from the leading scientists and science educators who serve on the STC Advisory Panel.

The STC project would not have been possible without the generous support of numerous federal agencies, private foundations, and corporations. Supporters include the National Science Foundation, the Smithsonian Institution, the U.S. Department of Defense, the U.S. Department of Education, the John D. and Catherine T. MacArthur Foundation, the Dow Chemical Company Foundation, the Amoco Foundation, Inc., E. I. du Pont de Nemours & Company, the Hewlett-Packard Company, and the Smithsonian Institution Educational Outreach Fund.

Acknowledgments

Balancing and Weighing was researched, developed, and written by Katherine Stiles in collaboration with the STC development and production team. The field-test edition was edited by Marilyn Fenichel and illustrated by Lois Sloan and Catherine Corder. The final edition was edited by Linda Harteker and illustrated by Lois Sloan, Jo Moore, and Heidi Kupke. The unit was trial taught in Amidon Elementary School in Washington, D.C.

The technical and educational review of *Balancing and Weighing* was conducted by:

Peter P. Afflerbach, Associate Professor, National Reading Research Center, University of Maryland, College Park, MD

Beverly Karplus Hartline, Associate Director and Project Manager, Continuous Electron Beam Accelerator Facility, Newport News, VA

Janet Kalin, Teacher, Valle Verde Elementary School, Concord, CA

Ramon Lopez, Director of Education and Outreach Programs, The American Physical Society, College Park, MD

Richard McQueen, Teacher/Learning Manager, Alpha High School, Gresham, OR

The unit was nationally field-tested in the following school sites with the cooperation of the individuals listed:

Hampton City Schools, Hampton, VA
Coordinator: Joyce Weeks, Math/Science Curriculum Leader
Patricia Fazzi, Teacher, Cooper Elementary School
Shirley Marhefka, Teacher, Phillips Elementary School
Cathy Robinson, Teacher, Bassette Elementary School

Highline School District, Seattle, WA
Coordinator: Judi Backman, Math/Science Coordinator
Sally Carlos, Teacher, North Hill Elementary School
Darci Downs, Teacher, Riverton Heights Elementary School
Darlene King, Teacher, Hazel Valley Elementary School

Mt. Diablo Unified School District, Concord, CA
Coordinator: Kathleen Jacobsen, Curriculum Specialist
Jinny Bergesen, Teacher, Meadow Homes Elementary School
Betsy DuRee, Teacher, Strandwood Elementary School
Janet Kalin, Teacher, Valle Verde Elementary School

West Seneca Central Schools, West Seneca, NY
Coordinator: John Cirrincione, Science Coordinator
Virginia Chatelle, Teacher, East Seneca Elementary School
Theresa Frankowski, Teacher, Potter Road Elementary School
Susan Murphy, Teacher, Northwood Elementary School

The NSRC also would like to thank the following individuals for their contributions to the unit:

Shari and Julie Argue, Burtonsville, MD. Julie is the gymnast whose story is featured in the reading selection in Lesson 3; Shari Argue is her mother.

Leslie J. Benton, Science Materials Consultant to Fairfax County Public Schools, Fairfax, VA

Brenda Collum, Science Coordinator, Amidon Elementary School, Washington, DC

Danielle Freese, Jane Freydenlund, and Marian Jackson, Teachers, Annandale Terrace Elementary School, Annandale, VA

Andrea Granston, Teacher, Amidon Elementary School, Washington, DC

Pauline Hamlette, Principal, Amidon Elementary School, Washington, DC

Eric F. Long, Staff Photographer, Special Assignments Branch, Office of Printing and Photographic Services, Smithsonian Institution, Washington, DC

Shawn Mallan, Program Coordinator, Volunteer and Education Service, National Zoological Park, Smithsonian Institution, Washington, DC

Mary Ellen McCaffrey, Photographic Production Control, Office of Printing and Photographic Services, Smithsonian Institution, Washington, DC

Mirsad Mehic, Owner and Director, Olympic Gymnastics, Inc., Silver Spring, MD

Dane Penland, Chief, Imaging and Technology Services Branch, Office of Printing and Photographic Services, Smithsonian Institution, Washington, DC

Sarah Sibbald, Office of Visual Services, National Gallery of Art, Washington, DC

Richard Strauss, Staff Photographer, Special Assignments Branch, Office of Printing and Photographic Services, Smithsonian Institution, Washington, DC

Robert Strawn, Photographer, Arlington, VA

The librarians and staff of the Central Reference Service, Smithsonian Institution Libraries, Washington, DC

STC Advisory Panel

STC Development and Production Team

Joyce Lowry Weiskopf, Project Director
Wendy Binder, Research Associate
Edward V. Lee, Research Associate
Christopher Lyon, Research Associate
Katherine Stiles, Research Associate
Amanda Revere, Office Assistant
Don Cammiso, Research Consultant
Carol O'Donnell, Research Consultant
Judy White, Research Consultant

Dean Trackman, Publications Director
Lynn Miller, Writer/Editor
Max-Karl Winkler, Illustrator
Heidi M. Kupke, Publications Technology Specialist
David Stein, Editorial Assistant
Laura Akgulian, Writer/Editor Consultant
Linda Harteker, Writer/Editor Consultant
Dorothy Sawicki, Writer/Editor Consultant
Lois Sloan, Illustrator Consultant

NSRC Administration

Douglas Lapp, Executive Director
Charles N. Hardy, Deputy Director for Information
    Dissemination, Materials Development, and
    Publications
Sally Goetz Shuler, Deputy Director for Development,
    External Relations, and Outreach
Diane Mann, Financial Officer
R. Gail Thomas, Administrative Officer
Gail Greenberg, Executive Administrative Assistant
Katherine Darke, Administrative Assistant
Karla Saunders, Administrative Assistant
Kathleen Holmay, Public Information Consultant

STC Evaluation Consultants

George Hein, Director, Program Evaluation and
    Research Group, Lesley College
Sabra Price, Senior Research Associate, Program
    Evaluation and Research Group, Lesley College

Contents

Goals for *Balancing and Weighing*

In this unit, students expand their understanding of the relationship between balance and weight as they explore activities in balancing, comparing, and weighing. Their experiences introduce them to the following concepts, skills, and attitudes.

Concepts

- Balance is affected by the amount of weight, the position of weight, and the position of the fulcrum.

- Weighing is the process of balancing an object against a certain number of standard units.

- The weight of an object is not determined by its size.

- Equal volumes of different foods will not all have equal weights; equal weights of different foods will not all have equal volumes.

Skills

- Performing simple experiments with balance.

- Applying previous experiences with balancing to build mobiles.

- Using an equal-arm balance to compare and weigh.

- Predicting the serial order for the weights of objects and foods.

- Applying strategies for comparing and weighing to solve problems.

- Recording results on record sheets, bar graphs, line plots, data tables, and Venn diagrams.

- Communicating ideas, observations, and experiences through writing, drawing, and discussion.

- Reading to learn more about balancing and weighing.

Attitudes

- Developing an interest in investigating balancing and weighing.

- Appreciating the importance of balancing and weighing in the everyday world.

- Accepting that a range of results is valid.

- Valuing the importance of simple scientific tools.

Unit Overview and Materials List

Many second-graders remember the challenge of balancing on two wheels when they began to ride a bicycle. Some may have gained an appreciation of the importance of balance as they watched a younger brother or sister learn to walk. Children experience balance in many other ways: riding a skateboard, participating in gymnastics, practicing ballet, or even walking on the curb on the way to school. Many children also show an interest in stacking blocks and in seeing how high they can build a tower before it topples over. All of these experiences lay the foundation for an understanding of how weight affects balance.

Balancing and Weighing, a 16-lesson unit for second-graders, provides activities that help children explore the relationship between balance and weight. They begin their investigations by exploring different ways to balance objects. They then examine different strategies for comparing objects. Later, they compare one object with a standard unit to determine its weight.

In the first five lessons, students explore balance through a number of activities, such as building structures, observing a beam balance, and creating mobiles. Students begin by describing their ideas about balance and how weight affects it. They then construct and explore a beam balance. They discover the important role that weight plays in balance and how a fulcrum can be moved to compensate for unequal or unevenly distributed weight. By the end of Lesson 4, students have been introduced to three variables that affect balance: the position of weight, the amount of weight, and the position of the fulcrum. They apply these concepts to the task of building mobiles in Lesson 5.

In Lessons 6 through 9, students begin to compare objects. To do so, they use a tool called the equal-arm balance. Unlike the beam balance, the equal-arm balance has a fixed fulcrum, allowing students to manipulate only weight. As students compare four and then six objects, they develop strategies for placing them in serial order from lightest to heaviest.

During Lesson 10, students discover that weighing is closely related to balancing; in fact, it is simply the process of balancing an object against a certain number of standard units. Students learn that they can weigh an object by placing the object in one pail of the equal-arm balance and adding Unifix Cubes™ to the other pail until the beam becomes level. In Lesson 11, students use information they recorded on a data table in Lesson 10 to make bar graphs that show the weight of each object.

In Lessons 12 through 15, the emphasis of the investigations changes. In this sequence of lessons, students apply their comparing and weighing skills to solve problems that involve four foods of varying weights, shapes, and sizes.

They begin these investigations by observing and describing the properties of four foods. They then compare and weigh cupfuls of the four foods. The students observe that even though the four empty cups were identical, they weigh different amounts when filled with the foods. In Lesson 15, students discover that equal weights of the four foods occupy different amounts of space.

Lesson 16, the culminating activity, challenges students to use the equal-arm balance to find out which of five containers holds a certain number of marbles. Solving this problem requires students to apply the various comparing and weighing strategies they have used throughout the unit and provides an embedded assessment of their progress.

The activities in this unit build on students' previous experiences with balance and weight and their intuitive understanding of this relationship. Through hands-on investigations and class discussions, students will not only find answers to many of their questions but also come up with new questions about balancing and weighing.

Following Lesson 16 is a post-unit assessment that is matched to the pre-unit assessment in Lesson 1. Additional assessments provide further questions and challenges for evaluating student progress.

Materials List

Below is a list of the materials needed for the *Balancing and Weighing* unit. Please note that the metric and English equivalents in this unit are approximate.

1	*Balancing and Weighing* Teacher's Guide
*30	optional Student Notebooks (*My Balancing and Weighing Book*)
30	new, unsharpened pencils (standard size), with erasers
30	jumbo paper clips
31	sheets of heavy orange paper, 67 lb, 22 × 28 cm (8½ × 11 in)
15	beam boards
15	fulcrums
62	squares of red construction paper, 10 cm (4 in) square
151	plastic drinking straws
15	boxes of No. 1 paper clips, 100 clips per box
15	sheets of red construction paper, 23 × 30.5 cm (9 × 12 in)
15	sheets of green construction paper, 23 × 30.5 cm (9 × 12 in)
15	sheets of blue construction paper, 23 × 30.5 cm (9 × 12 in)
15	sheets of yellow construction paper, 23 × 30.5 cm (9 × 12 in)
15	equal-arm balance support posts
15	equal-arm balance cross beams
15	equal-arm balance attachment pins
15	equal-arm balance bases
30	equal-arm balance S-hooks
30	equal-arm balance plastic pails, 1 liter (1 qt)
1	stick of clay
1	plastic knife
1	resealable plastic bag (for clay)
15	Ping-Pong balls
15	heavy-duty plastic spoons
15	wood blocks, 30 g (1 oz)
30	plastic cups, 296 ml (10 oz)
1	package of Plasti-Tak™
15	metal cubes, 60 g (2 oz)
15	acrylic cylinders, 2.5 cm diameter × 2.5 cm long (1 × 1 in)
2	Post-it™ pads, 76 mm (3 in) square (100 sheets per pad)
19	sheets of newsprint (for use in Lessons 8, 9, and 11), 61 × 91 cm (24 × 36 in)

60	plastic cups, 74 ml (2½ oz)
	Round oat cereal, 340 g (12 oz)
	Elbow macaroni, 680 g (1½ lb)
	Sunflower seeds (unsalted and in the shell), 450 g (1 lb)
	Split peas, 1.3 kg (2½ lb)
8	plastic pails with lids, 1 liter (1 qt)
30	red stick-on circles
30	green stick-on circles
30	blue stick-on circles
30	orange stick-on circles
15	yellow stick-on circles
1	red marker
1	blue marker
1	green marker
1	yellow marker
1	orange marker
390	glass marbles
75	film canisters with lids
150	red Unifix Cubes™
100	blue Unifix Cubes™
100	yellow Unifix Cubes™
100	green Unifix Cubes™
**	Scissors
**	Newsprint for all charts
**	Markers
**	Masking tape
**	Transparent tape
**	Student writing paper
**	Magnets
**	Glue or paste
**	Crayons
**	Transparent Con-Tact™ paper

*Note: The optional Student Notebooks are available from Carolina Biological Supply Company (1-800-334-5551).

**Note: These items are not included in the kit but are commonly available in most schools or can be brought from home.

Teaching *Balancing and Weighing*

The following information on unit structure, teaching strategies, materials, and assessment will help you give students the guidance they need to make the most of their hands-on experiences with this unit.

Unit Structure

How Lessons Are Organized in the Teacher's Guide: Each lesson in the *Balancing and Weighing* Teacher's Guide provides you with a brief overview, lesson objectives, key background information, a materials list, advance preparation instructions, step-by-step procedures, and helpful management tips. Many of the lessons include recommended guidelines for assessment. Lessons also frequently indicate opportunities for curriculum integration. Look for the following icons that highlight extension ideas:

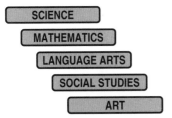

SCIENCE
MATHEMATICS
LANGUAGE ARTS
SOCIAL STUDIES
ART

Please note that all record sheets, blackline masters, student instructions, and reading selections may be copied and used in conjunction with the teaching of this unit.

Student Notebook: An optional consumable notebook, *My Balancing and Weighing Book*, has been published for this unit. The notebook is an individual, bound copy of all the record sheets, student instructions, and the three reading selections.

If your class does not use student notebooks, you will need to make copies of the record sheets, student instructions, and reading selections from the Teacher's Guide for your students, as directed in the individual lessons.

Students will use copies of blackline masters in four lessons of this unit: Lesson 1 (paper butterfly); Lessons 8 and 9 (objects for the serial order strips); and Lesson 11 (graph). Each one appears at the end of the lesson in which it is to be used. Blackline

masters are not included in the Student Notebook, so you will need to photocopy them for students.

Teaching Strategies

Classroom Discussion: Class discussions, effectively led by the teacher, are important vehicles for science learning. Research shows that the way questions are asked, as well as the time allowed for responses, can contribute to the quality of the discussion.

When you ask questions, think about what you want to achieve in the ensuing discussion. For example, open-ended questions, for which there is no one right answer, will encourage students to give creative and thoughtful answers. You can use other types of questions to encourage students to see specific relationships and contrasts or to help them to summarize and draw conclusions. It is good practice to mix these questions. It also is good practice always to give students "wait time" to answer; this will encourage broader participation and more thoughtful answers. You will want to monitor responses, looking for additional situations that invite students to formulate hypotheses, make generalizations, and explain how they arrived at a conclusion.

Brainstorming: Brainstorming is a whole-class exercise in which students contribute their thoughts about a particular idea or problem. When used to introduce a new science topic, it can be a stimulating and productive exercise. It also is a useful and efficient way for the teacher to find out what students know and think about a topic. As students learn the rules for brainstorming, they will become increasingly adept in their participation.

To begin a brainstorming session, define for students the topics about which they will share ideas. Tell students the following rules:

- Accept all ideas without judgment.

- Do not criticize or make unnecessary comments about the contributions of others.

- Try to connect your ideas to the ideas of others.

Figure T-1

Completed Venn diagram showing similarities and differences between the beam balance and the equal-arm balance

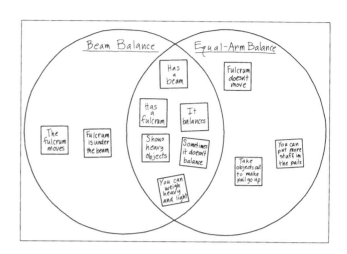

Venn Diagrams: Venn diagrams are useful tools for recording information to be compared. In this unit, you will use a Venn diagram to help students record their observations of the similarities and differences between the beam balance and the equal-arm balance.

Venn diagrams use circles to represent different sets of information. Figure T-1 illustrates a Venn diagram comparing the beam balance and the equal-arm balance. Words that describe the characteristics that are unique to each tool are recorded in the separate circles. The intersection of the circles contains the characteristics that are common to both tools.

Cooperative Learning Groups: One of the best ways to teach hands-on science is to arrange students in small groups. There are several advantages to this organization. It provides a small forum for students to express their ideas and get feedback. It also offers students a chance to learn from one another by sharing ideas, discoveries, and skills. With coaching, students can develop important interpersonal skills that will serve them well in all aspects of life. As students work, they will often find it productive to talk about what they are doing, resulting in a steady hum of conversation. If you or others in the school are accustomed to a quiet room, this new, busy atmosphere may require some adjustment.

Learning Centers: You can give supplemental science materials a permanent home in the classroom in a spot designated as the learning center. Students can use the center in a number of ways: as an "on your own" project center, as an observation post, as a trade-book reading nook, or simply as a place to spend unscheduled time when assignments are done. To keep interest in the center high, change the learning center or add to it often. Here are a few suggestions of items to include:

■ Science trade-books about balancing and weighing.

■ Audiovisual materials on related subjects.

■ Items contributed by students for sharing.

Materials

Organization of Materials: To help ensure an orderly progression through the unit, you will need to establish a system for storing and distributing materials. Being prepared is the key to success. Here are a few suggestions.

■ Read through the Materials List on pg. 4. Begin to collect the items you will need that are not provided in the kit.

■ Organize your students so that they are involved in distributing and returning materials. If you have an existing network of cooperative groups, delegate the responsibility to one member of each group.

■ Organize a distribution center and instruct your students to pick up and return supplies to that area. A cafeteria-style approach works especially well when there are large numbers of items to distribute.

■ Look at each lesson ahead of time. Some have specific suggestions for handling materials needed that day.

■ Become familiar with the safety tips that appear in some lessons.

- Management tips are also provided throughout the unit. Look for the icon at the right.

Safety: This unit does not contain anything of a highly toxic nature, but common sense dictates that nothing be put in the mouth. This includes the four foods that are used in Lessons 12 to 15. It is good practice to tell your students that, in science class, materials are never tasted.

Assessment

Philosophy: In the Science and Technology for Children program, assessment is an ongoing, integral part of instruction. Because assessment emerges naturally from the activities in the lessons, students are assessed in the same manner in which they are taught. They may, for example, perform experiments, record their observations, or make oral presentations. Such assessments permit the examination of processes as well as of products, emphasizing what students know and can do.

The learning goals in STC units include a number of different science concepts, skills, and attitudes. Therefore, a number of different strategies are provided to help you assess and document your students' progress toward the goals (see Figure T-2). These strategies also will help you report to parents and appraise your own teaching. In addition, the assessments will enable your students to view their own progress, reflect on their learning, and formulate further questions for investigation and research.

Figure T-2 summarizes the goals and assessment strategies for this unit. The left-hand column lists the individual goals for the *Balancing and Weighing* unit and the lessons in which they are addressed. The right-hand column identifies lessons containing assessment sections to which you can turn for specific assessment strategies. These strategies are summarized as bulleted items.

Assessment Strategies: The assessment strategies in STC units fall into three categories: matched pre- and post-unit assessments, embedded assessments, and additional assessments.

The first lesson of each STC unit is a *pre-unit assessment* designed to give you information about what the whole class and individual students already know about the unit's topic and what they want to find out. It often includes a brainstorming session during which students share their thoughts about the topic through exploring one or two basic questions. In the *post-unit assessment* following the final lesson, the class revisits the pre-unit assessment questions, giving you two sets of comparable data that indicate students' growth in knowledge and skills.

Throughout a unit, assessments are incorporated, or embedded, into lessons. These *embedded assessments* are activities that occur naturally within the context of both the individual lesson and the unit as a whole; they are often indistinguishable from instructional activities. By providing structured activities and guidelines for assessing students' progress and thinking, embedded assessments contribute to an ongoing, detailed profile of growth. In many STC units, the last lesson is an embedded assessment that challenges students to synthesize and apply concepts or skills from the unit.

Additional assessments can be used to determine students' understanding after the unit has been completed. In these assessments, students may work with materials to solve problems, conduct experiments, or interpret and organize data. In grades three through six, they may also complete self-assessments or paper-and-pencil tests. When you are selecting final assessments, consider using more than one to give students with different learning styles additional opportunities to express their knowledge and skills.

Documenting Student Performance: In STC units, assessment is based on your recorded observations, students' work products, and oral communication. All these documentation methods combine to give you a comprehensive picture of each student's growth.

Teachers' *observations and anecdotal notes* often provide the most useful information about students' understanding, especially in the early grades when some students are not yet writing their ideas fluently. Because it is important to document observations used for assessment, teachers frequently keep note cards, journals, or checklists. Many lessons include guidelines to help you focus your observations. The blackline master on pg. 11 provides a format you may want to use or adapt for recording observations. It includes this unit's goals for science concepts and skills.

Work products, which include both what students write and what they make, indicate students' progress toward the goals of the unit. Children produce a variety of written materials during a unit. Record sheets, which include written observations, drawings, graphs, tables,

continued on pg. 10

Balancing and Weighing: Goals and Assessment Strategies

Concepts	
Goals	**Assessment Strategies**
Balance is affected by the amount of weight, the position of weight, and the position of the fulcrum. Lessons 1–5	Lessons 1, 3, 4, and Additional Assessments 1–4 ▪ Pre- and post-unit assessments ▪ Class lists and charts ▪ Science journals ▪ Record sheets ▪ Class discussions ▪ Individual student conferences ▪ Teacher observations
Weighing is the process of balancing an object against a certain number of units. Lessons 10, 11, 14–16	Lessons 10, 12, and Additional Assessments 1, 3 ▪ Teacher's observations ▪ Class discussions ▪ Science journals ▪ Class lists and charts ▪ Individual student conferences
The weight of an object is not determined by its size. Lessons 7–15	Lesson 12 and Additional Assessment 3 ▪ Class discussions ▪ Science journals ▪ Individual student conferences
Equal volumes of different foods will not all have equal weights; equal weights of different foods will not all have equal volumes. Lessons 12–15	Lesson 12 and Additional Assessments 1, 3, 4 ▪ Class discussions ▪ Teacher observations ▪ Class lists and charts ▪ Record sheets ▪ Science journals ▪ Individual student conferences

Skills	
Goals	**Assessment Strategies**
Performing simple experiments with balance. Lessons 1, 3, 4	Lessons 1, 4, and Additional Assessments 2, 4 ▪ Pre- and post-unit assessments ▪ Teacher's observations ▪ Record sheets
Applying previous experiences with balancing to build mobiles. Lesson 5	Lesson 3 and Additional Assessment 1 ▪ Student product: mobile ▪ Class discussions ▪ Science journals
Using an equal-arm balance to compare and weigh. Lessons 6–10, 13–16	Lessons 6, 10, 12, 16, and Additional Assessments 3, 4 ▪ Teacher observations ▪ Class discussions ▪ Individual student conferences
Predicting the serial order for the weights of objects and foods. Lessons 8, 9, 13	Lessons 10, 12 ▪ Record sheets ▪ Class discussions ▪ Teacher observations

Skills *(continued)*

Goals	Assessment Strategies
Applying strategies for comparing and weighing to solve problems. Lessons 9, 15, 16	Lessons 6, 10, 12, 16, and Additional Assessment 4 • Teacher observations • Class discussions
Recording results on record sheets, bar graphs, line plots, data tables, and Venn diagrams. Lessons 3, 4, 6–14, 16	Lessons 1, 4, 6, 10, and Additional Assessments 2–4 • Pre- and post-unit assessments • Record sheets • Student products: bar graphs, serial order strips
Communicating ideas, observations, and experiences through writing, drawing, and discussions. Lessons 1–16	Lessons 1, 3, 4, 6, 10, 12, 16, and Additional Assessments 1–3 • Pre- and post-unit assessments • Class lists and charts • Class discussions • Record sheets • Science journals
Reading to learn more about balancing and weighing. Lessons 3, 5, 11	Lesson 3 and Additional Assessment 1 • Class discussions • Science journals

Attitudes	
Goals	**Assessment Strategies**
Developing an interest in investigating balancing and weighing. Lessons 1–16	Lesson 1 and Additional Assessment 3 • Pre- and post-unit assessments • Class discussions • Class lists and charts • Science journals • Teacher observations
Appreciating the importance of balancing and weighing in the everyday world. Lessons 2–5, 11	Additional Assessments 1, 3 • Class discussions • Class lists and charts • Science journals • Teacher observations
Accepting that a range of results is valid. Lessons 8, 10, 11, 14	Lessons 10, 12 • Class discussions • Class data tables and line plots • Teacher observations
Valuing the importance of simple scientific tools. Lessons 3, 4, 6–16	Lessons 1, 6, and Additional Assessment 1 • Pre- and post-unit assessments • Class discussions • Class charts and Venn diagram • Science journals • Individual student conferences

continued from pg. 7

and charts, are an important part of all STC units. They provide evidence of each student's ability to collect, record, and process information. Students' science journals are another type of work product. In grades one and two, journal writings are primarily suggested as extension activities in many lessons. Often a rich source of information for assessment, these journal writings reveal students' thoughts, ideas, and questions over time.

Students' written work products should be kept together in folders to document learning over the course of the unit. When students refer back to their work from previous lessons, they can reflect on their learning. In some cases, students do not write or draw well enough for their products to be used for assessment purposes, but their experiences do contribute to the development of scientific literacy.

Oral communication—what students say formally and informally in class and in individual sessions with you—is a particularly useful way to learn what students know. This unit provides your students with many opportunities to share and discuss their own ideas, observations, and opinions. Some young children may be experiencing such activities for the first time. Encourage students to participate in discussions, and stress that there are no right or wrong responses. Creating an environment in which students feel secure expressing their own ideas can stimulate rich and diverse discussions.

Individual and group presentations can give you insights about the meanings your students have assigned to procedures and concepts and about their confidence in their learning. In fact, a student's verbal description of a chart, experiment, or graph is frequently more useful for assessment than the product or results. Questions posed by other students following presentations provide yet another opportunity for you to gather information. Ongoing records of discussions and presentations should be a part of your documentation of students' learning.

Balancing and Weighing: Observations of Student Performance

STUDENT'S NAME:	

Concepts

Observations

- Balance is affected by the amount of weight, the position of weight, and the position of the fulcrum.

- Weighing is the process of balancing an object against a certain number of standard units.

- The weight of an object is not determined by its size.

- Equal volumes of different foods will not all have equal weights; equal weights of different foods will not all have equal volumes.

Skills

- Performing simple experiments with balance.

- Applying previous experiences with balancing to build mobiles.

- Using an equal-arm balance to compare and weigh.

- Predicting the serial order for the weights of objects and foods.

- Applying strategies for comparing and weighing to solve problems.

- Recording results on record sheets, bar graphs, line plots, data tables, and Venn diagrams.

- Communicating ideas, observations, and experiences through writing, drawing, and discussion.

- Reading to learn more about balancing and weighing.

| LESSON 1 | # Thinking about Balance |

Overview and Objectives

In this first lesson, students use simple materials to observe and explore the relationship between balance and weight. This activity provides you with a pre-unit assessment of your students' current knowledge of balancing. Students' entries in their science journals and the ideas they suggest for the class lists will give you further information about their baseline knowledge of balancing and questions they have about it. By comparing this information with parallel information that students will provide at the end of the unit, you will be able to assess the growth in each student's knowledge about balancing and the relationship between balance and weight. The activities in this lesson set the stage for Lesson 2, where students will investigate different ways of building structures that balance.

- Students balance a symmetrical object on a pencil.

- Students add weight to a symmetrical object and observe its effect on the object's balance.

- Students record what they know and questions they have about balancing.

- Students discuss their ideas about balancing.

Background

Most children in your class have already had experiences with balancing. Roller skating, riding a skateboard, riding a bicycle, and playing on a seesaw all require the ability to balance.

Many second-graders also have an intuitive sense that weight and the distribution of weight affect balance, but they may not have the vocabulary to explain this relationship. Their oral and written comments in this lesson will give you a sense of what they already know about balancing and the relationship between balance and weight. Students will have additional opportunities to investigate these subjects and build on their initial understanding throughout the rest of the unit. Comparing students' ideas from Lesson 1 with those they generate in the post-unit assessment will enable you to evaluate how their ideas have changed as a result of their classroom activities.

In order to assess students' progress at the end of the unit, you will want to save all the individual work products that students create during the lessons. These products will include record sheets, graphs, drawings, and science journals.

Materials

For each student

1   science journal

1   pair of scissors

1   new, unsharpened pencil (standard size), with eraser

For the class

1   copy of the blackline master **Figure of a Butterfly**

31 sheets of heavy orange paper

30 jumbo paper clips

2   sheets of newsprint

1   marker

Note: The newsprint sheets provided in the *Balancing and Weighing* kit are intended for use in Lessons 8, 9, and 11, not for the charts you will create throughout the unit. You will need your own supply of newsprint sheets for the charts.

Preparation

1. On one sheet of newsprint, write the title "What We Know about Balancing." On the second sheet, write "What We Would Like to Know about Balancing." Write the current date on both sheets.

2. Using the heavy orange paper, make 31 copies of the blackline master **Figure of a Butterfly** (pg. 17). Cut out one butterfly for your own use.

3. Decide what to use for the students' science journals. Standard composition books, notebook paper in folders, or blank pages that have been bound work well. Every student will need his or her own science journal for the pre- and post-unit assessment activities. In addition, most lessons in the unit contain extensions that suggest ways students can use the science journals to record their ideas about the activities conducted during the lesson.

4. Create space for a distribution center that will contain all the materials needed for each lesson except those that you will distribute yourself (see Figure 1-1). Before each lesson, assemble the materials and arrange them

Figure 1-1

Distribution center

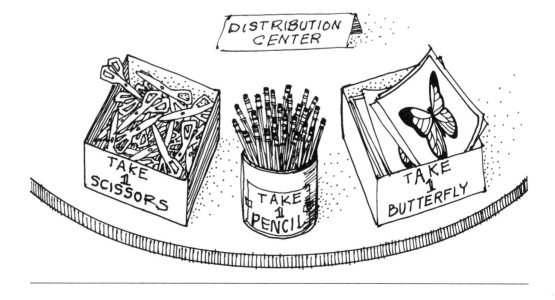

Figure 1-2

Balancing the butterflies

"cafeteria style." Then have students pick up each item they need. To set up an efficient distribution center, follow the guidelines listed below.

- Select one large area or several small areas of the room.

- Arrange the materials in separate containers. Shoe boxes work well. Place a label on each container that indicates what it holds and how many items the students should take.

- Place all the materials in a line on several desks or tables that have been pushed together.

- Be sure there is enough space for students to easily walk by in a single file on both sides of the supplies.

Procedure

1. Show students the butterfly that you copied and cut out. Ask them to suggest different ways they could balance it on a pencil.

2. Let students know that they will now have a chance to balance their own butterflies. Have each student go to the distribution center and collect one butterfly copied on orange paper, a pair of scissors, and an unsharpened pencil.

3. Ask students to cut out the butterfly. Then give them time to explore balancing the butterfly. Encourage them to try as many different ways as possible.

4. Ask a few students to share how they balanced the butterfly. Encourage students to describe why it balances.

5. Distribute a jumbo paper clip to each student. Challenge students to attach the paper clip to various places on the butterfly and to find new ways to balance it.

6. Ask students to share their observations of how the butterfly balanced this time. Encourage them to describe why the paper clip changed how the butterfly balanced.

Final Activities

1. Distribute the science journals. Ask each student to write his or her ideas in response to the statement "What I know about balancing." After a few minutes, ask students to write the questions they have about balancing.

2. Display the chart entitled "What We Know about Balancing." Invite students to share some of the ideas they wrote in their journals. Record them on the chart.

3. Now focus students' attention on the chart entitled "What We Would Like to Know about Balancing." Again, ask students to share ideas from their science journals and record them on the chart.

4. Let students know that during the next few weeks they will be investigating balancing and weighing. At the end of this time, they will look at the chart again to see which questions they have answered.

    Note: Save both pre-assessment charts for use in the post-unit assessment.

Extensions

    SCIENCE

1. In a learning center, have students balance an odd-shaped piece of cardboard on a tennis ball that has been cut in half. Challenge them to place washers or Unifix Cubes™ on top of the cardboard and to try to keep it balanced. Encourage students to draw and write about what they discover.

    SCIENCE

2. Copy illustrations of various animals on heavy paper and cut them out. Challenge students to find ways of balancing the cutouts on a pencil or ruler. The butterfly is symmetrical, which makes balancing easier. Consider using animals that are asymmetrical.

Assessment

In the section entitled Teaching *Balancing and Weighing* on pgs. 5–11, you will find a detailed discussion about the assessment of students' learning. Specific goals and related assessments for this unit are summarized in Figure T-2: *Balancing and Weighing:* Goals and Assessment Strategies on pgs. 8–9.

The two brainstorming charts used in Lesson 1, "What We Know about Balancing" and "What We Would Like to Know about Balancing," are the first half of a matched pre- and post-unit assessment. The second half appears in the post-unit assessment on pgs. 147–148. Both are important components of your assessment of student growth and learning.

Students' writings about what they observe and discover can provide evidence of the progression of their ideas. These written comments will also alert you to students' questions and give you insight into topics in which they are especially interested. You may want to periodically review your students' science journals or conduct individual "science meetings" that give each student an opportunity to share some of the ideas he or she has written about.

Figure of a Butterfly

Building Structures that Balance

Overview and Objectives

In this lesson, students build structures that balance using a beam, a fulcrum, and Unifix Cubes™. Creating towers, walls, bridges, and other types of structure provides an opportunity for students to make new observations about balancing and to become familiar with the materials they will use in upcoming lessons. As students share their experiences building these structures, they enhance their descriptive skills. Students will apply many of the observations they make today in Lesson 3, when they construct and explore a beam balance.

- Students build structures that balance.

- Students describe their structures and share their observations about balancing.

- Students discuss balancing and weighing in the world around them.

Background

Weight and how it is distributed, which we will call distance, interact to affect how an object balances. The effect of weight is easy to observe. Think, for example, of a seesaw. Adding or removing weight affects the way the plank, or beam, balances. Distance, the second factor affecting balance, is defined as the length of the interval between the weight and the fulcrum. A **fulcrum** is a support upon which a beam balances or pivots; in Lesson 1, the fulcrum was a pencil. Distance may be manipulated by placing the weight at various positions along the beam or by changing the position of the fulcrum. Weight and distance may also be altered in combination; for example, you may simultaneously place different amounts of weight on the beam at different distances from the fulcrum.

In this unit, students will explore the interactions between weight and distance. They will change weight by adding Unifix Cubes™ to or removing them from the beam; they will change distance by varying the position of the Unifix Cubes™ and the position of the fulcrum. For ease of reference, you will present the activities of upcoming lessons to your students in terms of exploring the effects of three variables: amount of weight, position of weight, and position of the fulcrum.

This lesson sets the stage for students' future explorations by giving them an opportunity to investigate various ways that a beam, a fulcrum, and Unifix Cubes™ may be combined to create balanced structures. Each type of structure provides the chance to discover something new and different about balancing. For example, students who build bridgelike structures may discover that the supports do not always have to be at the very ends of the bridge. The appropriate position for the supports may be virtually anywhere beneath the bridge, depending on the position of the weight on top. Students who create seesaws may discover that they can make the beam level even when it has a different number of Unifix Cubes™ on each end, provided they place the fulcrum in the appropriate position. Students who build towers may discover ways to balance the Unifix Cubes™ to create very tall structures.

Materials

For every two students
- 1 beam
- 1 fulcrum
- 20 Unifix Cubes™

For the class
- 1 sheet of newsprint
- 1 marker

Preparation

1. On the sheet of newsprint, write the title "Ways We Balance and Weigh."

2. Arrange the materials in the distribution center. One way to distribute the Unifix Cubes™ efficiently is to connect them into sticks of 10 and to place each color in a separate container.

3. Students will work in pairs in this lesson. If necessary, rearrange the tables or desks so that students have enough work space.

Procedure

1. Point out the materials in the distribution center. Let students know they will use them to build structures that balance.

2. Divide students into pairs. Have one member of each pair collect a fulcrum, a beam, and 20 Unifix Cubes™ from the distribution center.

Figure 2-1

Building structures that balance

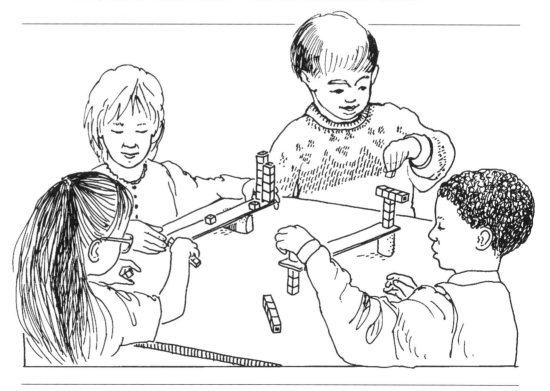

3. Ask students to build their structures. To help students focus on how their structures are balancing, ask them some of the following questions as they work:

- What could you remove from your structure and still have it balance?

- Why would your structure fall over if I removed this piece?

- Where could you add Unifix Cubes™ to your structure without making it become unbalanced?

- If you wanted to make the structure fall over, where would you add Unifix Cubes™?

4. When they have completed their structures, ask students to leave them on their desks.

Final Activities

1. Invite students to describe their structures. Encourage them to discuss what they discovered while building them. To facilitate this discussion, you may want to ask individual students some of the questions from Step 3 in the **Procedures** section.

2. Ask students to dismantle their structures and return the materials to the distribution center.

3. Then display the chart "Ways We Balance and Weigh." As students brainstorm ideas, record them on the chart. Figure 2-2 shows some ideas you might expect from your students.

4. Keep the chart on display and encourage students to add ideas to it during the next few weeks.

Figure 2-2

Students' ideas about balancing and weighing

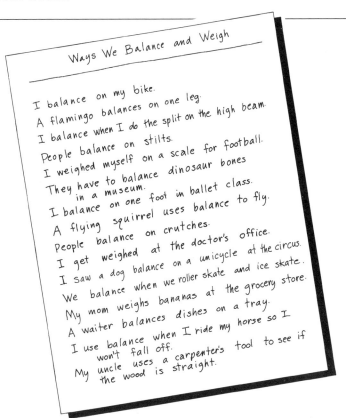

Ways We Balance and Weigh

I balance on my bike.
A flamingo balances on one leg.
I balance when I do the split on the high beam.
People balance on stilts.
I weighed myself on a scale for football.
They have to balance dinosaur bones in a museum.
I balance on one foot in ballet class.
A flying squirrel uses balance to fly.
People balance on crutches.
I get weighed at the doctor's office.
I saw a dog balance on a unicycle at the circus.
We balance when we roller skate and ice skate.
My mom weighs bananas at the grocery store.
A waiter balances dishes on a tray.
I use balance when I ride my horse so I won't fall off.
My uncle uses a carpenter's tool to see if the wood is straight.

Figure 2-3

*Student
illustration*

Joi Nash

Extensions

ART

1. Have students illustrate the ideas you have recorded on the "Ways We Balance and Weigh" chart. Use the illustrations to make a bulletin board or bind them to create a class book. Figure 2-3 shows an example of a student illustration.

LANGUAGE ARTS

2. Encourage students to create their own list of "Ways We Balance and Weigh" in their science journals. Suggest that they include examples of activities that occur outside of school, such as getting weighed at the doctor's office, weighing vegetables in the supermarket, riding a skateboard, and watching acrobats at the circus.

SCIENCE

3. Suggest that students explore other ways of balancing. The Bibliography (pgs. 155–157) contains descriptions of several books that your students can use to help them build things that balance and explore other activities that involve balancing.

Exploring the Beam Balance

Overview and Objectives

In Lesson 2, students began to investigate the relationship between balance and weight as they used Unifix Cubes™, a fulcrum, and a beam to create balanced structures. In this lesson, they discover how changing the amount of weight (the number of Unifix Cubes™) and the position of weight (the location of the Unifix Cubes™ on the beam) affect the way a beam balances on a fulcrum. By reading about a young gymnast, students connect their discoveries about balance and weight to a real-life experience.

- Students build a beam balance.

- Students explore how the amount of weight and position of weight affect balance.

- Students discuss the various ways they were able to balance the beam.

- Students read about a seven-year-old gymnast.

Background

Today, your students will build a beam balance. They will then explore ways they can manipulate the Unifix Cubes™ to balance the beam. In Lesson 4, they will explore the same problem by moving the fulcrum. To prepare for this lesson and those that follow, you may want to experiment with the beam balance.

When the fulcrum is directly under the center of the beam and the beam does not have any Unifix Cubes™ on it, the beam balances. This is because the weight of the beam is evenly distributed on each side of the fulcrum. If you place an equal number of Unifix Cubes™ on each end of the beam, as shown in Figure 3-1, the beam will remain in equilibrium.

Figure 3-1

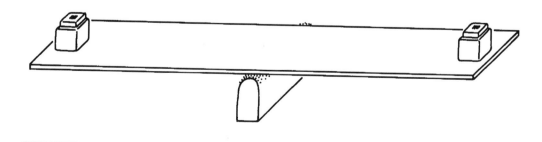

But what happens if you move the fulcrum? The empty beam will not balance. If the fulcrum is closer to the left end of the beam, the right end of the beam will tilt downward. If you place the Unifix Cubes™ in appropriate positions, however, you can balance the beam when the fulcrum is off center.

Suppose you were given 10 Unifix Cubes™ and challenged to balance the beam with the fulcrum off center. Once you started to explore, you would find that the problem could be solved in a number of ways. You might place all 10 cubes on one end of the beam, as shown in Figure 3-2.

Figure 3-2

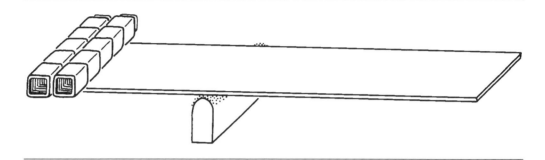

You might also place nine cubes on the left end of the beam and one cube near the right end, as shown in Figure 3-3.

Figure 3-3

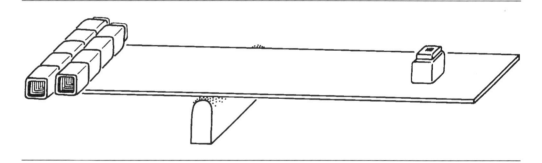

Or you could place eight cubes on the left end and the other two on the right, close to the fulcrum, as shown in Figure 3-4.

Figure 3-4

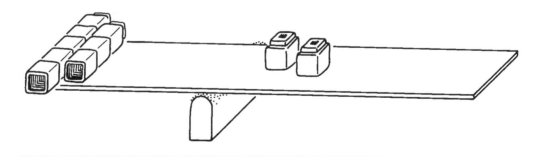

If you moved the fulcrum in either direction, you would have to change the number and position of the Unifix Cubes™ in order to keep the beam level. It is this intricate interrelationship between amount of weight, position of weight, and position of the fulcrum that students will explore during the next two lessons.

Materials

For each student

1   copy of **Record Sheet 3-A: Beam Balance Discoveries**
1   copy of "Julie's Balancing Act"

For every two students

1   fulcrum
1   beam
10   Unifix Cubes™

For the class

1   sheet of newsprint
1   marker

Note: *My Balancing and Weighing Book*, the student notebook, contains all the record sheets, student instructions, and reading selections used in this unit. If your class is not using the student notebook, you will need to photocopy these pages for your students. All items that you must photocopy appear in the teacher's guide at the end of the lesson in which they will be used.

Preparation

1.   Make one copy of **Record Sheet 3-A: Beam Balance Discoveries** (pg. 32) for each student.

2.   Make one copy of "Julie's Balancing Act" (pgs. 33–35) for each student.

3.   Arrange the materials in the distribution center. Figure 3-5 illustrates one way of setting up the distribution center for this lesson.

Figure 3-5

Distribution center

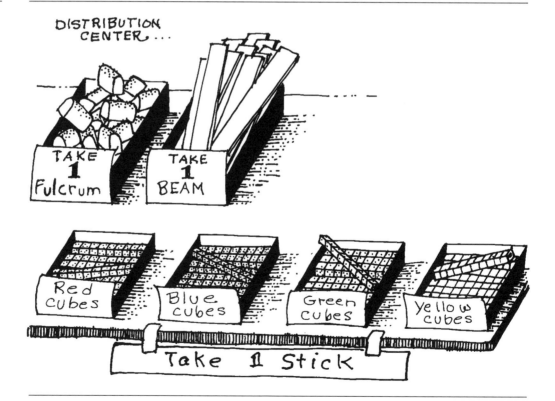

4. At the top of the sheet of newsprint, write the title "Balancing the Beam." Under the title, draw a picture of the beam balanced on the fulcrum, as illustrated in Figure 3-6.

Figure 3-6

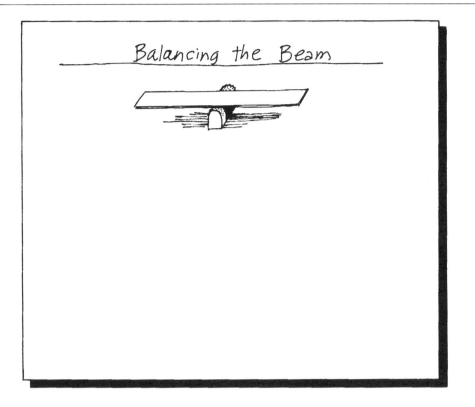

Procedure

1. Ask students to describe how they used their materials in Lesson 2 to create balanced structures. Then display an assembled beam balance with the fulcrum under the center of the beam. Let students know that this structure is called a beam balance and that today they will build their own beam balances.

2. Before students begin, invite them to discuss what might happen when weight—Unifix Cubes™—is added to the beam balance. Record these ideas on the "Balancing the Beam" chart.

3. Have students pick up their materials from the distribution center and build their beam balances.

4. Once the balances are assembled, have students explore what happens when they place the Unifix Cubes™ on the beam. Encourage them to place the cubes in various positions on each side of the beam.

5. Distribute **Record Sheet 3-A: Beam Balance Discoveries** and have students draw and write about two discoveries they made.

6. After students complete the record sheets, have them return their materials to the distribution center.

Figure 3-7

Exploring the beam balance

Final Activities

1. Conduct a discussion about the students' discoveries. The following questions may help guide this discussion:

   ■ How did you make the beam balance?

   ■ When would the beam not balance?

   ■ What did you discover when you put the Unifix Cubes™ in different places on the beam?

2. To help students recognize that a fulcrum is any support on which an object balances, discuss the similarities between the materials they used in this lesson and those used in Lesson 1. Use the following questions to begin this discussion:

   ■ Is the fulcrum more like the pencil or the butterfly? How?

   ■ Is the beam more like the pencil or the butterfly? How?

   ■ Describe the similarities and differences between balancing the butterfly by adding a paper clip and balancing the beam by adding Unifix Cubes™.

3. Introduce the reading selection by asking students to discuss how a gymnast might use balance to walk on a beam.

4. Distribute a copy of "Julie's Balancing Act" to each student. Read the story to the class or have students read it aloud in pairs or silently to themselves.

5. Ask students to discuss the following questions:

- Have you ever taken gymnastics classes?

- Did you ever walk a balance beam? What did you do to keep your balance?

- Have you ever watched a ballet? How do you think a ballerina stays on her toes?

- In addition to gymnastics and ballet, what other activities require the ability to balance?

Extensions

SCIENCE

1. Obtain a board and fulcrum large enough so that a student can stand on each end. Have students repeat the activities from this lesson using themselves, instead of Unifix Cubes™, as weights.

SCIENCE

2. Have students bring in games or toys that rely on balance, such as Jenga™ or Blockhead™. Have them identify and discuss the equivalents of the fulcrum and beam in each game.

LANGUAGE ARTS

3. Have students take home their copies of "Julie's Balancing Act" to share with their families.

LANGUAGE ARTS

4. Have students write in their science journals about what they are discovering. Creating specific questions or open-ended sentences can be helpful for young writers. Below are a few writing ideas.

- Write directions for building a beam balance.

- Today I discovered _____.

- Write down the names of three things that are balanced, such as a chair. How do you think it stays balanced? What could you do to make it fall over?

Assessment

This lesson is the first in a series of three lessons in which students explore how the amount of weight, the position of weight, and the position of the fulcrum affect balance. Listed here are some suggestions to use during these three lessons for assessing your students' understanding of the role that each of these variables plays in balance.

Lesson 3

- Do students effectively manipulate the beam and Unifix Cubes™ to create balance?

- Do students describe the way the Unifix Cubes™ change how the beam balances? Do they discuss the position of the weight? The amount of weight?

Lesson 4

- Do students describe where to place the fulcrum under the beam to make it balance?

- Do students describe how the beam can balance when they place a different number of Unifix Cubes™ on each end?

- Do students relate their discoveries concerning the beam balance to help explain what happened when they tried to balance the butterfly and paper clip?

Lesson 5

- Do students manipulate the paper clips, straws, and construction paper to make simple mobiles?

- Do students explain how and why their mobiles balance?

- What modifications in the position of the fulcrum do students make if the mobile leans to one side?

- Do students change the amount of weight, position of weight, or both, to help create balance?

- Do students identify fulcrum points in the photograph of Alexander Calder's mobile?

Record Sheet 3-A

Name: _____

Date: _____

Beam Balance Discoveries

Draw two ways you balanced the beam.

Julie's Balancing Act

There's no place that seven-year-old Julie Argue would rather be than in the gym. And the gymnastics activity she likes best is walking on the balance beam. In fact, Julie could walk the balance beam before she could ride a bicycle!

Julie is a second-grader. She started taking gymnastics classes when she was five. She now spends nine hours a week at the gym. Julie hurries home from school. Homework comes first, and then a quick dinner. After that, it's off to the gym!

Each gymnastics lesson begins with warm-up exercises. Then, Julie and the other girls in her class practice on the balance beam. When Julie and her friends started out, they used a beam that was 15 centimeters (about 6 inches) off the ground. Then they practiced on a beam that was twice as high. Once their coach knew they were ready, Julie and her friends began to work out on a beam like the one that older gymnasts use in competition. That beam is 120 centimeters—about 4 feet—high.

Julie can walk backwards and forwards on the beam. She can also do flips. She even can make a full turn on one foot! How does Julie keep her balance? "The trick is to use my arms," she says. "Sometimes I move them out to the sides. Sometimes I move them backward or forward."

You can see this when you watch Julie perform. If she tips to the left, she moves her right arm up. If she starts to tip backward, her arms move forward. By moving her arm in the opposite direction each time she starts to tilt, Julie shifts the position of her weight and remains in balance.

Julie has learned another important trick from her coach: "I look straight ahead—at the end of the beam—not down." The coach, Mirsad Mehic, says with a smile, "Keep your eyes on your toes, and you'll fall on your nose."

In addition to walking the balance beam, Julie does floor exercises. She also practices on the uneven bars and the vault. These are the same exercises done by gymnasts in the Olympic Games.

Is there an Olympic medal in Julie's future? Maybe. She's now old enough to enter local competitions. But for now, her mother says, there's something more important. Julie's having a great time!

Photos: Robert Allen Strawn

LESSON 4	# Moving the Fulcrum

Overview and Objectives

In the last lesson, students observed that the amount of weight and the position of weight affect how a beam balances on a fulcrum. In this lesson, they explore the third variable that affects balance: the position of the fulcrum. Students will discover that they can make the beam balance, even though the weight it supports is uneven or unevenly distributed, by changing the position of the fulcrum. In Lesson 5, students will apply what they have discovered about the relationship between balance and weight as they design and create mobiles.

■ Students balance a beam with Unifix Cubes™ by changing the position of the fulcrum.

■ Students describe and compare their observations.

■ Students record their results.

■ Students add their observations of balancing and weighing in the world around them to the class list.

Background

In Lesson 3, your students discovered various ways of balancing a beam with Unifix Cubes™ when the fulcrum remained in the center of the beam. Today, students focus on a new question: What happens when they move the fulcrum?

To review the concepts that students will explore in this lesson, you may wish to reread the **Background** for Lesson 3. The same principles apply in this lesson; however, the variable that students now will manipulate is the position of the fulcrum.

Materials

For each student
1   copy of **Record Sheet 4-A: Where Is the Fulcrum?**

For every two students
1   fulcrum
1   beam
20   Unifix Cubes™

For the class
1   copy of the blackline master **Beam Balances**
1   sheet of newsprint
1   marker

"Ways We Balance and Weigh" chart (from Lesson 2)
Tape or glue

Preparation

1. Make one copy of **Record Sheet 4-A: Where Is the Fulcrum?** (pg. 41) for each student.

2. Arrange the materials in a distribution center.

3. At the top of the sheet of newsprint, write the title "The Fulcrum and Beam." Make one copy of the blackline master **Beam Balances** (pg. 42). Cut out each of the beam balance figures. Glue or tape them to the chart, as illustrated in Figure 4-1.

Figure 4-1

Procedure

1. Ask students to briefly discuss what they discovered about how to make the beam balance in Lesson 3.

2. Display the chart "The Fulcrum and Beam." Describe what students will do in this lesson.

   ■ Each student will receive a record sheet that shows the same beam balance figures that are on the chart.

   ■ Working in pairs, they will place the Unifix Cubes™ on the beam in the ways shown on the record sheet.

   ■ They will slide the beam across the fulcrum to find the spot where the beam becomes level.

■ Each student will record this position on his or her own record sheet.

Note: It is difficult to move the fulcrum under a beam that is holding Unifix Cubes™. For this reason, you will ask the students to slide the beam across the fulcrum rather than to actually move the fulcrum. Let students know, however, that it is the position of the fulcrum that they should focus on when they make their observations and record their results.

3. Distribute copies of **Record Sheet 4-A: Where Is the Fulcrum?** Have students collect materials from the distribution center and begin the activity.

4. Make sure that each student indicates the position of the fulcrum on each figure shown on the record sheet.

5. After students have completed the activity, have them return the materials to the distribution center.

Figure 4-2

Arranging the Unifix Cubes™

Final Activities

1. Ask students to discuss where they placed the fulcrum for each of the examples. Record their responses on the chart "The Fulcrum and Beam" by drawing the fulcrum beneath each beam.

2. Discuss some of the students' findings. The following suggestions may help guide the discussion:

■ Point to one example on the chart. Why is the fulcrum in this spot? Why does the beam balance when the fulcrum is here?

■ Why do you think the beam can balance with an uneven number of cubes on the ends?

■ What did you discover today that could help explain why you had to move the pencil after you added a paper clip to the butterfly?

3. Ask students to look at the "Ways We Balance and Weigh" chart and add any new ideas. Then encourage students to select one idea from the chart and to discuss how distribution of weight might affect the balance of an object or a person. For example, students might suggest that skateboarders sometimes need to lean to one side to stay balanced.

4. Save the students' record sheets for use in an additional assessment after the unit is completed.

Extensions

SCIENCE

1. In the learning center, provide a box of miscellaneous items and a beam balance. Have students place various objects on the beam and slide the beam across the fulcrum until it balances. Then encourage them to investigate what happens when they move the objects instead of the fulcrum.

SCIENCE

2. Have students walk on a beam or curb. Then ask them to discuss questions such as the following:

   ■ How did you keep your balance?

   ■ What did you do with your arms to help you walk along the beam?

   Now ask them to carry a heavy object as they walk on the beam or curb. How does this affect their balance?

LANGUAGE ARTS

3. Suggest that students read a book such as *Mirette on the High Wire*, by Emily Arnold McCully (see Bibliography). The story is about a young girl's friendship with a famous tightrope walker.

LANGUAGE ARTS

4. Have students continue to write in their science journals. Some ideas for sentence starters include the following:

   ■ I was surprised by (or when) _____.

   ■ I found out that _____.

   ■ I think the fulcrum is important because _____.

SCIENCE

5. Make one copy of the blackline master **Balancing at the Circus** on pg. 43 for each student. Have students discuss the various ways they see the performers and animals balancing.

Assessment

In **Additional Assessment 2** (pg. 150), you will ask students to perform an activity similar to the one in this lesson and to complete record sheets that show their results. Save students' completed copies of **Record Sheet 4-A: Where Is the Fulcrum?** A comparison of this record sheet with the one from the additional assessment will help you assess each student's growth.

Record Sheet 4-A

Name: -

Date: -

Where Is the Fulcrum?

Draw the fulcrum to show how the beam balanced.

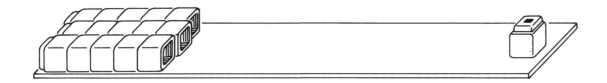

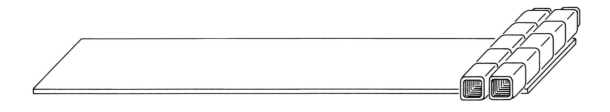

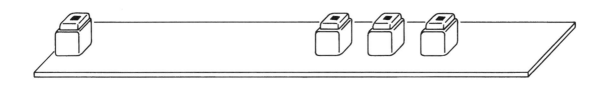

Beam Balances

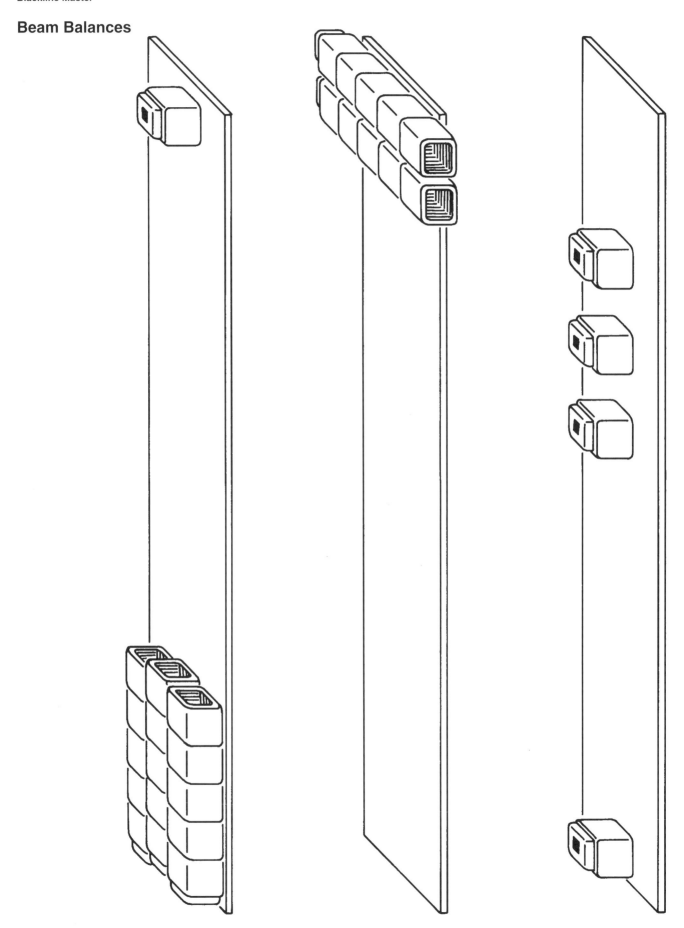

Balancing at the Circus

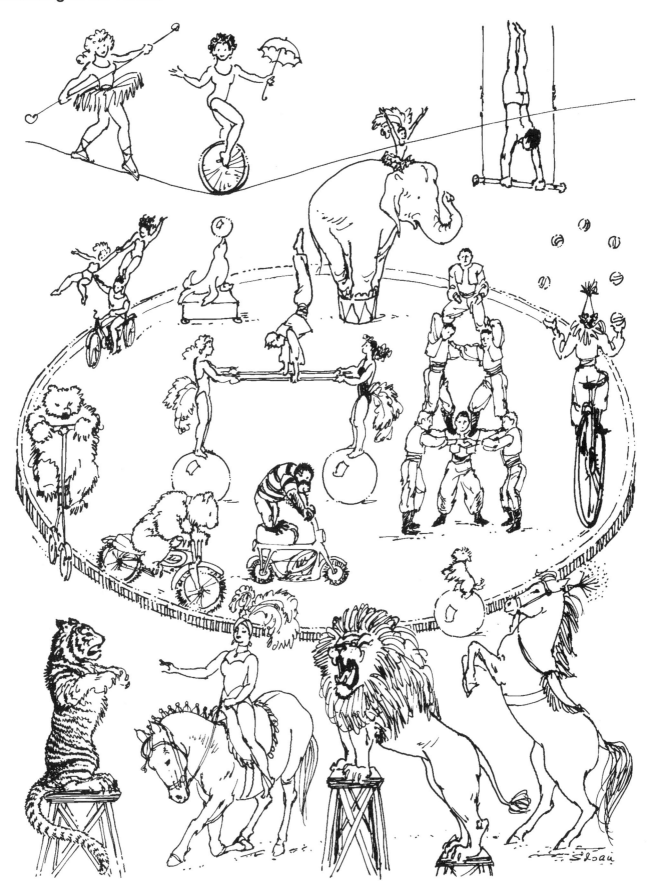

LESSON 5

Building Mobiles

Overview and Objectives

Making mobiles offers students an opportunity to apply what they have discovered about the relationship between balance and weight. Students discover that they can design mobiles with various fulcrum points and that they can change the balance of a mobile by adding a small amount of weight or by shifting its position slightly. For many children, this lesson will also be an introduction to a fascinating art form and to a famous artist, Alexander Calder, whose mobiles hang in museums around the world.

■ Students build simple mobiles that balance.

■ Students describe and compare how their mobiles balance.

■ Students construct more complex mobiles.

■ Students read about Alexander Calder, the "mobile man."

Background

When most people hear the word "mobile," they envision intricate, slowly moving structures suspended in the air. Some mobiles are small and lightweight, while others are huge. All of them have specially designed parts that enable them to remain balanced. They have support rods of varying lengths that serve as the beams. The objects hung from these rods are the weights. The amount of weight, its position, and the position of the fulcrum points determine how the mobiles balance.

As your students construct their mobiles, they will be manipulating all of these variables. They may observe that the mobile, unlike the beam balance, may have several fulcrum points. Some students may note that the weight is supported from above rather than from below. Designing these creations is a practical application of students' growing understanding of the relationship between balance and weight.

Materials

For every two students

  2   pairs of scissors

  4   pieces of red construction paper, 10 cm (4 in) square

  2   support beams with paper clip chains taped on the end

  1   box of No. 1 paper clips

10   straws

  4   sheets of construction paper (one each of red, yellow, green, and blue)

For the class
1 straw
2 pieces of red construction paper, 10 cm (4 in) square
1 sheet of newsprint
1 marker
   Several paper clips
   Masking tape

Management Tip: Preparing the materials for this lesson may take more time than usual. You may want to invite parent volunteers or older students from another class to help you.

Preparation

1. On the sheet of newsprint, write the title "Balancing Mobiles."

2. Make one copy of "Alexander Calder: The Mobile Man" (pgs. 51–53) for each student.

3. Using one straw, two squares of red construction paper, and several paper clips, build a mobile. Figure 5-1 illustrates an example of a simple mobile.

4. To provide one support beam for each student, use the 15 beams from the beam balance and the 15 cross beams from the equal-arm balance.

Figure 5-1

A simple mobile

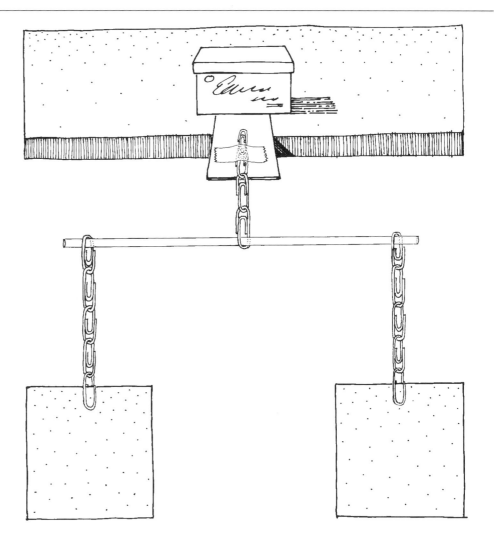

5. Connect four paper clips for each student. With the masking tape, attach one end of the paper clip chain to one end of the support beam. Figure 5-2 shows a completed support beam.

Figure 5–2

*Completed
support beam*

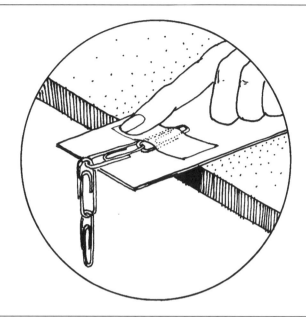

6. Select a convenient method for securing the support beams at students' desks. Two suggested methods are illustrated in Figure 5-3. You may, for example, place the end of the beam on the top of a desk or table, with the end of the paper clip chain extending over the edge. Then stack books on the other end of the beam to hold it in place. If the desks in your classroom have open fronts, you can ask students to slide the beam into the opening and anchor it with heavy objects. Students will probably need to sit on the floor to have easy access to their mobiles.

Figure 5–3

*Two ways to
anchor the
support beam*

Figure 5–4

*Distribution
center*

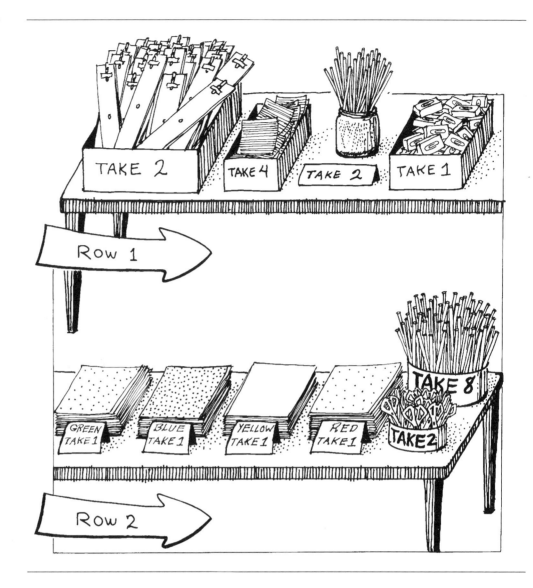

7. Arrange the materials in the distribution center, as illustrated in Figure 5-4. Students will use the materials in the top row during the first activity when they build simple mobiles. Later, they will use the materials in the bottom row to construct more intricate mobiles.

Procedure

1. Introduce the lesson by asking students to share what they know about mobiles. Because some students may never have seen a mobile, display the one that you made. Then let students know that they will build their own mobiles.

2. Describe how students can anchor their support beams at their desks. Then have one student from each pair collect the following materials from the distribution center:

   ■ 2 support beams

   ■ 4 squares of red construction paper

   ■ 2 straws

   ■ 1 box of paper clips

3. Challenge each student to use these materials to build a simple mobile.

Management Tip: If the students' paper clips slide off the straw, advise them to attach the smaller end of the paper clip to the straw, as shown in Figure 5-5. You may also need to demonstrate how to connect the paper clips to form a chain. Finally, let students know that they should attach the construction paper to the paper clips without bending them out of shape. For safety reasons, you probably will not want students to straighten the clips or use them as hooks.

Figure 5–5

Securing the paper clips to the straws

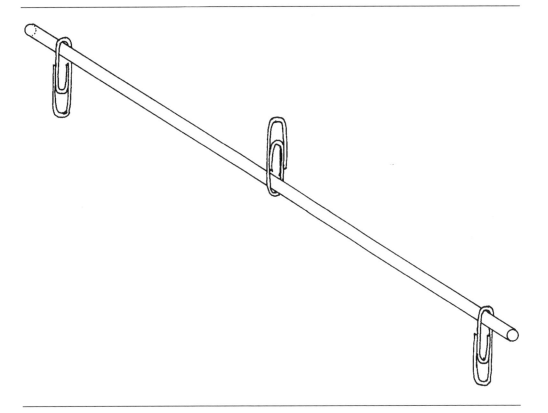

4. After students have completed their mobiles, ask them to describe why and how their mobiles balance. Record their responses on the chart "Balancing Mobiles." The following questions may help guide the discussion:

    ■ How does the mobile stay balanced?

    ■ What part of the mobile is like the beam?

    ■ What part of the mobile is like the fulcrum?

    ■ Where is the weight on the mobile?

5. Have each pair of students collect materials from the second row of the distribution center. Remind students that each pair needs to share the straws, construction paper, and paper clips. Now invite them to make more elaborate mobiles.

Final Activities

1. After students have completed their mobiles, discuss questions such as the following:

   ■ How did you change your mobile?

   ■ What did you add? What did you remove?

   ■ Does it still balance?

2. Remove the mobiles from the support beams and tape them in a convenient place. Have students return the support beams, scissors, and any unused materials to the distribution center.

3. Distribute a copy of "Alexander Calder: The Mobile Man" to each student. Have them follow along as you read the story or ask them to read it alone silently or aloud in pairs.

4. Have students take their mobiles and the reading selection home to share with their families.

Extensions

SCIENCE

1. Suggest that students combine their mobiles. Two or more students could attach their mobiles; students could even create a huge class mobile made up of everyone's mobile.

ART

2. Have students make mobiles that reflect themes they are studying, such as plants or animals, or that use objects found on a nature walk. Students could also create mobiles that reflect their own hobbies or interests.

LANGUAGE ARTS

3. Encourage students to continue writing in their science journals. Have them draw pictures of the mobiles they made in this lesson and write about how they balance.

LANGUAGE ARTS

4. Consult the Bibliography (pgs. 155–157) for resources on Alexander Calder and photographs of his work. Challenge students to find fulcrums, beams, and weights in the photographs of Calder's mobiles. After they look at the photographs, they may be inspired to create more elaborate mobiles of their own.

Alexander Calder: The Mobile Man

Do you know what you want to be
when you grow up? Some people do.
Alexander Calder was one of those people.
He was born in 1898, and from the time he
was a boy, he knew he wanted to be an artist.

Alexander, or Sandy to his friends, always liked
to make things. When he was only five years old,
he used wood and wire to make statues of people
and animals. When he was eight, he began making
jewelry. Using beads and copper wire, he created
jewelry for his sister Peggy's dolls.

Even when he grew up, Sandy Calder loved toys
and dolls and animals. He once made a tiny circus.
From metal, wood, cloth, and paper, Calder made
acrobats who could swing through the air and
elephants that could blow water from rubber trunks.
Today, you can see Calder's circus at a museum
in New York City.

Sandy continued to work on his art.
He grew to love bright colors like red and blue.
He liked to use simple shapes like rectangles and
circles. He wondered if he could figure out a way to
make these shapes move. So he invented mobiles,
which could hang in the air and "dance with the joy
of life and surprises." By the time Calder died in
1976, people all over the world were enjoying
his new form of art.

When you made your mobiles in this lesson,
you had to figure out how to create a balance.
So did Sandy Calder. He worked hard, cutting
out shapes, arranging them, and attaching
them so that each one balanced the other.
He was pleased if his mobiles moved in the
breeze or made interesting shadows.

Here is a drawing of one of Sandy Calder's
mobiles. Can you pick out the fulcrums
and the weights? Calder's mobiles are
perfectly balanced.

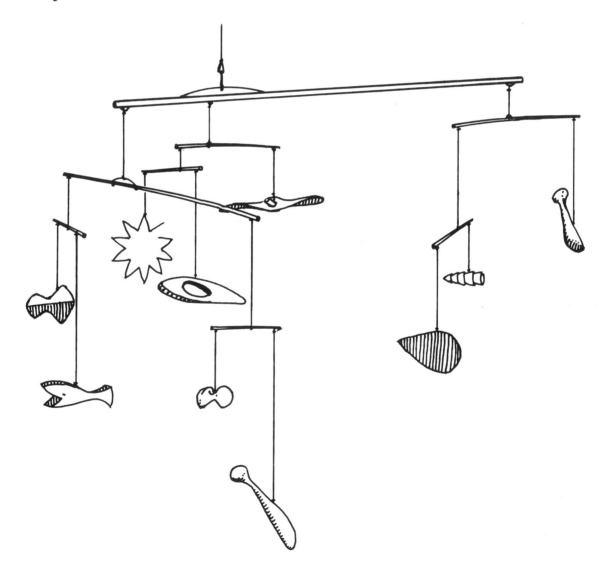

One of Calder's most famous mobiles, which hangs in the National Gallery of Art in Washington, D.C., is bigger than a school bus! When people enter the museum, this beautiful red, black, and blue mobile is one of the first things they see.

Here is a photograph of that mobile. Can you pick out the fulcrums and the weights? How might it move in the air?

Alexander Calder, *Untitled,* 1976. Gift of the Collectors Committee, © 1994 Board of Trustees, National Gallery of Art, Washington, D.C.

Exploring the Equal-Arm Balance

Overview and Objectives

Students have now examined the three variables that affect balance: amount of weight, position of weight, and position of the fulcrum. In this lesson, they have an opportunity to apply what they have discovered about the beam balance as they begin to work with an equal-arm balance. Using free exploration, students discover what happens when they place a variety of objects in the pails of the equal-arm balance. Through discussion, they compare and contrast the equal-arm balance and the beam balance. In upcoming lessons, students will use the equal-arm balance to compare and weigh objects.

■ Students assemble and equilibrate an equal-arm balance.

■ Students observe and describe how the equal-arm balance reacts when they place objects in the pails.

■ Students compare and contrast the equal-arm balance and the beam balance and record their observations on a class Venn diagram.

Background

The equal-arm balance is similar to the beam balance in many ways. Each has a fulcrum and a beam, and weights can be added to the beams. There are, however, two important differences between the tools. First, the fulcrum of the equal-arm balance, unlike that of the beam balance, is in a fixed position. A second difference is position of the weights. Weights may be placed at any position along the beam balance. With the equal-arm balance, by contrast, the position of the weights is constant—they are placed in pails suspended from each end of the cross beam. Figure 6-1 shows the similarities between the beam balance and the equal-arm balance.

You can expect students to put almost everything in sight into the pails of the equal-arm balance during this lesson! This free exploration, during which they add, remove, and interchange objects between the pails, gives students the opportunity to figure out how the equal-arm balance works. This introductory experience is important because students will use the equal-arm balance throughout the remainder of this unit.

Figure 6-1

*The beam balance
and the equal-arm
balance*

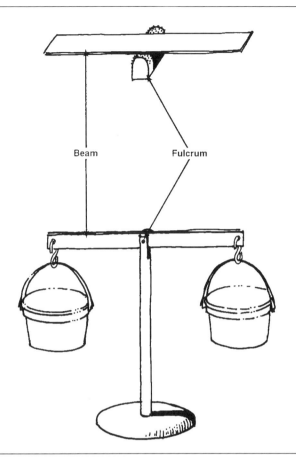

Materials

For every two students

1   copy of **Student Instructions for Assembling the Equal-Arm Balance**
2   plastic pails, 1 liter (1 qt)
2   S-hooks
1   support post
1   cross beam
1   attachment pin
1   base
     Miscellaneous objects from students' desks

For the class

1   beam balance
2   sheets of newsprint
1   marker
1   resealable plastic bag
1   stick of clay
1   plastic knife
30   Post-it™ notes, 76 mm (3 in) square
1   roll of masking tape
     Transparent tape

Preparation

1. This is a long lesson. Review the **Procedures,** then decide if you want to conduct all the activities in one lesson or if you prefer to schedule two class periods. One natural breaking point is the **Final Activities,** which you might even want to teach during mathematics.

2. Make one copy of **Student Instructions for Assembling the Equal-Arm Balance,** on pg. 63, for every two students.

3. Slice the stick of clay into 16 pieces.

4. Assemble one equal-arm balance according to the student instructions. If the cross beam tilts, place a small piece of clay on it in order to level, or **equilibrate,** the beam.

5. Allocate space for storage of the 15 equal-arm balances.

6. To create the Venn diagram, tape together two sheets of newsprint along the longer side. Then draw two overlapping circles on the newsprint. Label one circle "Beam Balance" and the other circle "Equal-Arm Balance," as illustrated in Figure 6-2.

Figure 6-2

Labeled circles of the Venn diagram

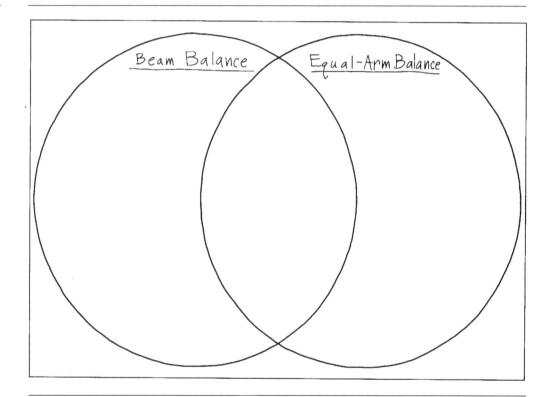

Procedure

1. Display a beam balance. Ask students to discuss with their partners what they know about the beam balance.

2. Distribute one Post-it™ note to every two students and have them write one thing they know about the beam balance on it. Then ask them to stick the Post-it™ note to the Venn diagram in the circle labeled "Beam Balance."

3. Now introduce students to their new tool, the equal-arm balance, by displaying the one that you assembled.

4. Let the students know that they will assemble their own equal-arm balances. Distribute a copy of **Student Instructions for Assembling the Equal-Arm Balance** to each pair of students. Let them know they may use these instructions, as well as the equal-arm balance you have displayed, to help them.

5. Have students collect the materials needed for the equal-arm balances. While they are assembling the balances, distribute a piece of masking tape to every two students. Ask students to write their names on the tape and stick it to the base of the balance.

6. After students have assembled their equal-arm balances, ask them to describe the differences and similarities among them. Students may notice that some beams are level and some are not. If students do not raise this observation themselves, alert them to it by focusing their attention on two balances—one whose cross beam is level and one whose beam is clearly tilted.

7. Let students know that leveling the cross beam is an important step in assembling the equal-arm balance. Distribute the pieces of clay and ask students to use them to level the cross beams.

Figure 6–3

Leveling the equal-arm balance

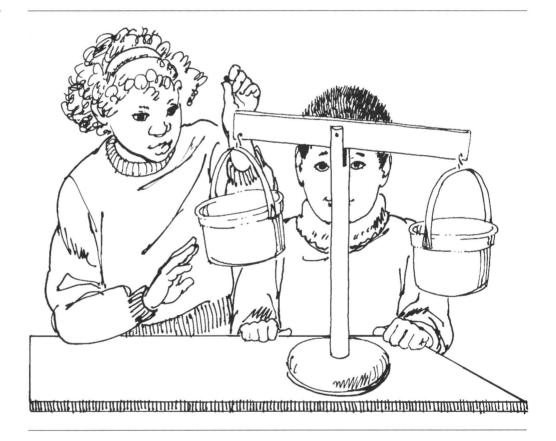

 Management Tip: Encourage students to use tiny pieces of clay and to add them to one side of the cross beam at a time. If the beam does not equilibrate after they have added clay to one side, suggest that they either add clay to the other side or remove a small amount of clay from the first side.

8. Once the equal-arm balances are equilibrated, have students use materials from their desks to explore what happens when they place objects in the pails. Encourage them to place various combinations of objects in the pails.

Figure 6–4

Exploring with the equal-arm balance

9. After 5 or 10 minutes, focus students' continued explorations by asking some of the following questions:

    ■ What can you do to make one pail move down?

    ■ What can you do to make one pail move up?

    ■ What can you do to make the two pails level?

10. Have students place the equal-arm balances in the storage area. They should leave the clay on the beam. Ask them to place any leftover clay in the resealable plastic bag.

Final Activities

1. Ask students to discuss with their partners what they have observed about the equal-arm balance.

2. Distribute another Post-it™ note to every two students and have them record one observation about the equal-arm balance on it. Then ask them to stick the note in the circle on the Venn diagram labeled "Equal-Arm Balance." Figure 6-5 illustrates an example of a Venn diagram with some comments you might expect from your students.

Figure 6-5

Venn diagram with student comments in both circles

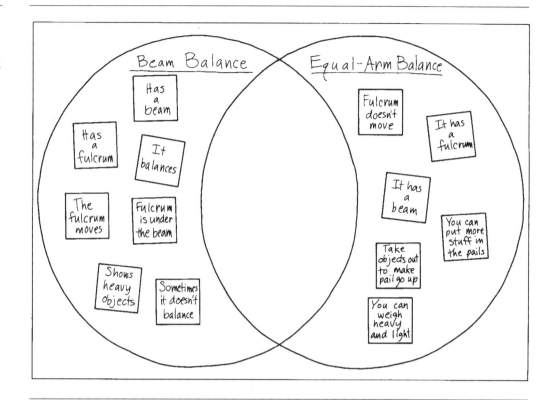

3. Initiate a class discussion to help students compare their observations about the beam balance and the equal-arm balance. Begin by focusing on characteristics the two tools have in common. For example, both have a beam, and adding weight makes one side of the beam move down.

4. As students identify the similarities, move the appropriate Post-it™ notes to the area where the circles of the Venn diagram overlap. A completed Venn diagram is illustrated in Figure 6-6.

5. Now ask students to identify the differences between the equal-arm balance and the beam balance. To help students make this comparison, encourage them to focus on the comments that remain in the two outer sections of the two circles of the Venn diagram.

6. Leave the Venn diagram on display. Students may discover new ideas that they will want to add in future lessons.

Extensions

MATHEMATICS   SOCIAL STUDIES

1. Bring a carpenter's level to class. Ask students to discuss how it works and how a carpenter might use it.

SOCIAL STUDIES

2. Let students know that people in some countries of the world carry water in buckets over their shoulders on structures that resemble the equal-arm balance. Ask them to discuss why it might be easier to carry two buckets of water than just one bucket.

Figure 6-6

Completed Venn
diagram

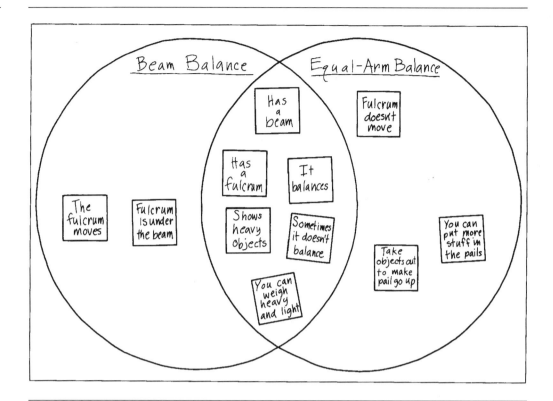

Beam Balance   Equal-Arm Balance

Has a beam

Fulcrum doesn't move

Has a fulcrum   It balances

The fulcrum moves   Fulcrum is under the beam   Shows heavy objects   Sometimes it doesn't balance   Take objects out to make pail go up   You can put more stuff in the pails

You can weigh heavy and light

SCIENCE

3. Challenge students to add a third circle to the Venn diagram that compares the mobile with the beam balance and the equal-arm balance. Or have students create a Venn diagram to show the relationship between the mobile and the butterfly from Lesson 1.

LANGUAGE ARTS

4. Have students draw a picture of the equal-arm balance and then write about it in their science journals. They may find these sentence starters helpful.

■ One pail moved down when I added _____.

■ I made the pails level by _____.

■ The equal-arm balance is like the beam balance because _____.

Assessment

This lesson is the first in a series of four lessons in which students explore how to use the equal-arm balance to compare objects. The following guidelines may help you assess your students' progress during these lessons.

Lesson 6

■ What characteristics of the beam balance do students list?

■ How do students apply what they discovered in Lessons 1 to 5? For example, if a child immediately adds clay to the higher side of the cross beam, this may mean that he or she understands how to compensate for the weight difference in order to create balance.

■ What techniques do students use to level the pails? Do they add objects? Remove objects? Move objects from one pail to the other?

- What characteristics of the equal-arm balance do students list?

- Listen for comments that show students' understanding that characteristics moved to the intersection of the Venn diagram are common to both balances.

- Listen for comments that show students' understanding that the characteristics remaining in the outer sections of the two circles of the Venn diagram are unique to each balance.

Lessons 7, 8, and 9

Knowledge of the Equal-Arm Balance

- What strategies do students use to determine which objects are "heavier than" or "lighter than" others?

- How do students decide if two objects are "equal to" each other?

Comparing Objects

- How do students compare four objects? Six objects?

- What strategies do students apply to compare the objects and arrange them in serial order?

- What conclusions do students make about objects A and C when comparing objects A and B and C?

- Are students able to articulate that if A > B, then B < A?

- Do students' comments reflect an understanding of the importance of fair comparisons?

Student Instructions for Assembling the Equal-Arm Balance

1. Slide one S-hook into the hole at each end of the beam.

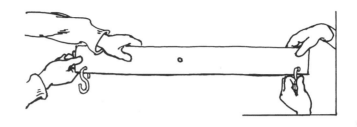

2. Twist the post into the round base.

3. Place the cross beam in the slot at the top of the post. Make sure the S-hooks are hanging down.

4. Have your partner slide the pin into the hole at the top of the post. Make sure the pin also goes through the hole in the cross beam.

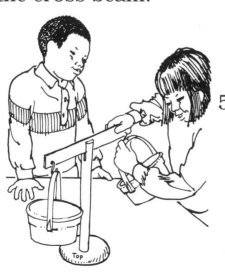

5. Hang the pails on the S-hooks. There is a hole in the handle of each pail. Slide the S-hook into this hole.

Using the Equal-Arm Balance to Compare Objects

Overview and Objectives

In this lesson, students deepen their understanding of the uses of the equal-arm balance as they place a variety of objects in the pails and observe and compare the results. This activity provides an opportunity to discuss the idea of fair comparisons. Students will refine and apply the problem-solving strategies they begin to develop in this lesson throughout the rest of the unit. In Lesson 8, for example, they will use the results of their comparisons to place four objects in serial order.

- Students use the equal-arm balance to compare objects.

- Students record comparisons using binary symbols—greater than (>), less than (<), and equal to (=).

- Students discuss their comparisons and problem-solving strategies.

- Students discuss the concept of fair comparisons.

Background

In this lesson, students begin to compare objects using the equal-arm balance. They discover that if one pail moves down, its contents are heavier than those of the other pail. This reaction also indicates that the contents of the higher pail are lighter than those of the lower pail. If the cross beam remains level with a different object in each pail, those objects are equal. Later in the unit, students will discover that such objects have the same weight.

At this age, students often focus on the heavier of the two objects when making comparisons. For example, they might say only that "the book is heavier than the pencil." Recognizing that A is heavier than B **and** that B is lighter than A is part of learning how to make comparisons. Although this seems obvious to adults, it may not be initially apparent to your students. Drawing conclusions about lightness or heaviness requires that students not only observe whether the pails move up or down but also understand why they do so.

Materials

For every two students
2 copies of **Record Sheet 7-A: Comparing Objects**
1 assembled equal-arm balance
1 piece of clay
6 miscellaneous objects from students' desks

For the class
  2 sheets of newsprint
  1 marker

Preparation

1. Make one copy of **Record Sheet 7-A: Comparing Objects** (pg. 69) for each student.

2. On one sheet of newsprint, write the title "Comparing Objects."

3. Save the second sheet of newsprint to record students' comments during Step 1 of the **Final Activities.**

Procedure

1. Ask students to describe what happened when they placed objects in the pails of the equal-arm balance in Lesson 6.

2. Let them know that today they will use the equal-arm balance to compare objects from their desks. To make their comparisons, students will need to place only one object in each pail at a time, as illustrated in Figure 7-1.

Figure 7-1

Comparing objects with the equal-arm balance and recording results

3. Distribute a copy of **Record Sheet 7-A: Comparing Objects** to each student. Review the directions on the sheet, pointing out the box that highlights the binary symbols. Let students know that they will use these symbols to record their observations.

4. Ask students to collect the equal-arm balances and clay. If the beam tilts, have them equilibrate it with clay. Remind the students that they should always level the cross beam before they use the equal-arm balance.

5. Invite each pair of students to select six objects from their desks that they would like to compare. Remind them to compare only two objects at a time and to record their comparisons on the record sheets.

6. After students have completed their comparisons, ask them to return the equal-arm balances to the storage area. Ask them to keep the record sheets at their desks to refer to during the discussion.

Final Activities

1. Ask each student to select one comparison from the record sheets that he or she would like to share with the class. Use binary symbols to record these comparisons on the chart "Comparing Objects," as illustrated in Figure 7-2. Encourage each student to emphasize the relationship between the two objects by stating his or her comparison in two ways. For example, if the student first states that "the eraser > the paper," he or she should then be encouraged to note that "the paper < the eraser."

Figure 7-2

Recording results of student comparisons

2. Using student observations that you have recorded on the chart as examples, invite students to discuss the following issues:

■ Describe how you decided that _____ was lighter than/heavier than _____.

■ Describe what you observed on the equal-arm balance that helped you decide that _____ was heavier than/ lighter than _____. Did you look at the cross beam? The pails?

Note: Although your students probably will be eager to describe the exact comparisons they made and what they discovered about the objects, it may be difficult for them to explain the strategies they used to make these comparisons. Encourage them to rephrase their comments in a way that clearly describes the process they went through to decide an object was lighter than, heavier than, or equal to another object.

3. Ask students why it was important to level the cross beam before making comparisons. You might want to highlight the following ideas about fair comparisons:

■ If all the equal-arm balances are level at the beginning of the activity, the results of comparisons of two objects will be the same, regardless of which balance you use.

■ If the cross beam of the balance is level, the pails are also level. The pails "start out even," just like runners who begin a race from the same starting line. As a result, a comparison of two objects will reflect the true difference between them.

Extensions

SCIENCE

1. Create a learning center where students can compare additional objects on the equal-arm balance. Students could write task cards for each other to compare various objects, such as "Is the crayon [>, <, or =] the pencil?"

SCIENCE

2. In a learning center, provide challenges for students to solve, such as "How could you use the equal-arm balance to equally share a box of raisins with one person? With three people?"

MATHEMATICS

3. Have students create number sentences to help them connect their use of binary symbols in this lesson to their studies in mathematics. For example, have students determine whether the "greater than" or "less than" symbol should be used in number sentences, such as "7 is (< or >) 2 + 3."

LANGUAGE ARTS

4. Have students write in their science journals. Ask them to list words that are used to compare objects, such as "heavier than," "bigger than," and "wider than." Or ask them to list synonyms for "heavy" and "light."

LANGUAGE ARTS

5. Invite students to write a riddle using descriptive words that compare size and weight. Here is an example of a problem-solving riddle.

"I am smaller than a lunch box. I am bigger than a crayon. I am lighter than a book. I am heavier than a sheet of paper. I keep your fingers from getting cold in the snow. What am I?"

Record Sheet 7-A

Name: -

Date: -

Comparing Objects

> Heavier than
< Lighter than
= Equal to

On each line, write the names of the objects you compared.
Write one symbol that shows the comparison.

1. _____ _____ _____
(>, <, =)

2. _____ _____ _____
(>, <, =)

3. _____ _____ _____
(>, <, =)

4. _____ _____ _____
(>, <, =)

Developing Strategies for Placing Objects in Serial Order

Overview and Objectives

In the first six lessons, students explored and extended their understanding of balance. In the last lesson, the focus shifted to using balance to compare objects. Lesson 8 now challenges students to apply their comparing skills to develop strategies for placing objects in serial order from lightest to heaviest. To formulate their strategies, students compare four objects—a Ping-Pong ball, a plastic spoon, a plastic cup, and a wood block—using the equal-arm balance. In Lesson 9, they will continue to refine their strategies by comparing six objects.

- Students predict the serial order, from lightest to heaviest, of four objects.

- Students use the equal-arm balance to help them place four objects in serial order from lightest to heaviest.

- Students record the serial order of the objects and discuss the relationships among them.

- Students describe the strategies they devised to place the four objects in serial order.

Background

Putting objects in serial order can be challenging for young children. It requires the ability to compare three or more objects and to recognize the relationship of each object to the others. A child who has mastered this developmental concept, called **transitivity,** understands that if object A is heavier than object B and object B is heavier than object C, then object A is also heavier than object C. In other words, $A > B > C$.

Your students probably will approach the task of placing objects in serial order in a concrete way. For example, they may first compare the plastic cup with the block. After noting that the block is heavier, they may replace the cup with the spoon and observe that the block is also heavier than the spoon. Discovering these relationships requires students to make a sequence of comparisons, carefully observe and record the results, and draw conclusions.

Your students may not all obtain the same results. Some may conclude, for example, that the spoon is lighter than the Ping-Pong ball. These two objects are very close in weight, and slight differences in the way they are manufactured may make their weights even closer. You may wish to discuss these issues with your students.

Materials

For each student
1 copy of the blackline master **The Four Objects**
1 sheet of writing paper
1 pair of scissors

For every two students
1 assembled equal-arm balance
1 piece of clay
1 plastic cup, 296 ml (10 oz)
1 Ping-Pong ball
1 plastic spoon
1 wood block
1 square of Plasti-Tak™ adhesive

For the class
1 copy of the blackline master **Teacher's Objects**
5 sheets of newsprint
1 marker
   Plasti-Tak™ adhesive or masking tape
4 magnets (optional)

Preparation

1. Make enough copies of the blackline master **The Four Objects,** on pg. 80, so that each student has one set of pictures of the four objects.

2. On one sheet of newsprint, write the title "From Lightest to Heaviest."

3. Using the remaining four sheets of newsprint, make one strip of newsprint for each student.

    ■ Fold a sheet of newsprint in half along the longer side.

    ■ Now fold the sheet in half in the same direction two more times. After you have made all three folds, cut the sheet into eight strips, each measuring approximately 61 × 11 cm (24 × 4½ in). A paper cutter may make this task easier.

    ■ Repeat these steps with the remaining three sheets of newsprint.

4. Using a pair of scissors, cut the Plasti-Tak™ into 15 pieces.

5. Make a copy of the blackline master **Teacher's Objects,** on pgs. 78–79. Cut out the six pictures. You will use only four pictures in this lesson—the Ping-Pong ball, plastic spoon, wood block, and plastic cup. You will use the metal cube and acrylic cylinder for the first time in Lesson 9. Because the pictures will be used repeatedly in subsequent lessons, you may want to cover them with transparent Con-Tact™ paper or laminate them.

6. Arrange the materials in a two-part distribution center, placing the Ping-Pong balls, plastic spoons, and wood blocks in the plastic cups. Figure 8-1 illustrates one way to set up the materials.

Figure 8-1

Distribution center

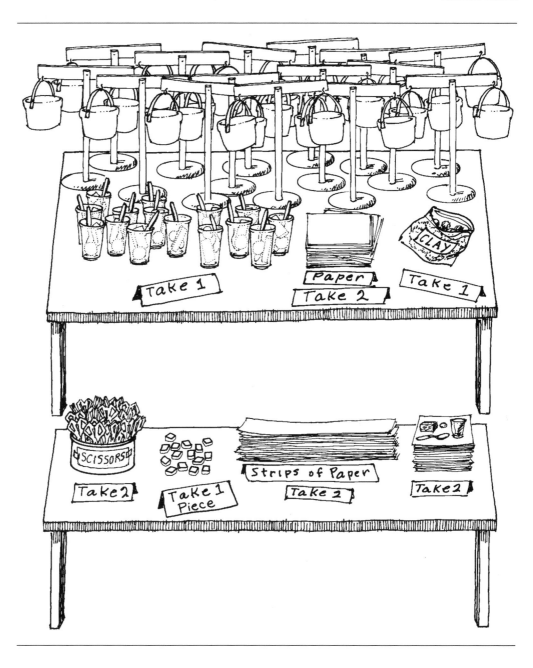

Procedure

1. Ask students to review the strategies they used in the last lesson to compare objects. If some students placed objects in serial order at that time, encourage them to describe the approaches they used.

2. Have one student from each pair collect the four objects and two sheets of writing paper from the distribution center. Ask students to hold each of the objects and then to predict a serial order from lightest to heaviest.

3. Have students write their predictions for the serial order of the objects on a sheet of paper.

4. Ask students to collect the equal-arm balances and clay. Give them a few minutes to equilibrate the balances.

5. Now have students use the equal-arm balance to compare the four objects and to arrange them in serial order.

Figure 8-2

*Predicting a
serial order*

6. If some students are not sure how to proceed, encourage them to talk with other students about their strategies. You also can ask prompting questions, such as "What do you know about the object if the pail moves down?" or "How can you use what you observe about the two pails to decide which object is heavier?" Figure 8-3 shows one student's drawing of the sequence of comparisons he made.

7. Once students have finished, ask them to place the objects on their desks from left to right, beginning with the lightest object, in the serial order they have determined.

Final Activities

1. Ask students to return their balances to the distribution center and to pick up the scissors, pieces of Plasti-Tak™, strips of newsprint, and copies of the blackline master **The Four Objects.**

2. Have students cut out the pictures. Then have them use the Plasti-Tak™ to attach the pictures left to right, from lightest to heaviest, to the strip of newsprint, as shown in Figure 8-4. You may want to let students know that they are using this special adhesive because they will need to move their pictures in the next lesson.

3. After students have affixed the cutouts to the strips, ask them to write their names on the strips. Then have them return all their materials except the strips to the distribution center.

Figure 8-3

Student
illustration

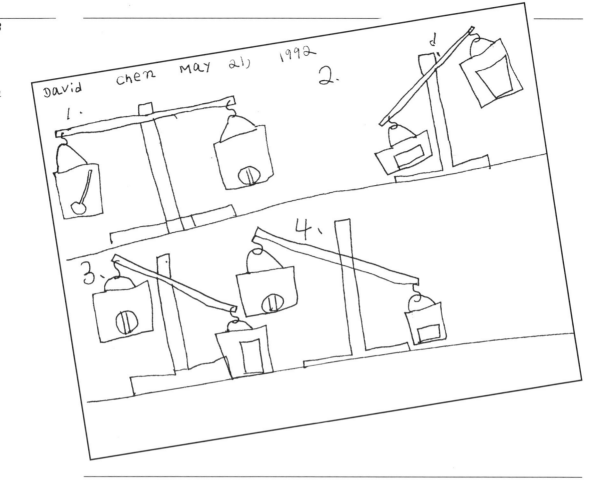

Figure 8-4

Placing the cutouts
in serial order

4. Have students describe the order of the objects on their strips. Then ask them to discuss how their results are different from or the same as their predictions. The following questions may help students think about and verbalize the steps they took to compare the objects:

   ■ When you decided what object was the lightest, what was in the other pail?

   ■ How did you decide which object was the heaviest?

   Note: Students may decide on different serial orders for the objects. If this happens, ask them to discuss possible reasons for the differences.

5. During this discussion, use the sheet of newsprint titled "From Lightest to Heaviest" to show the serial order of the four objects. Attach your four cutouts to the newsprint using tape or Plasti-Tak™.

Management Tip: If your classroom has magnetic blackboards, you can use magnets to secure the cutouts.

6. Write binary symbols to show the relationship of each object to the one next to it, as illustrated in Figure 8-5. If students want to write these symbols on their strips, have them do so in pencil, because they will add two objects to the strips in Lesson 9.

7. Collect the strips and save them for Lesson 9.

Figure 8-5

Discussing the results of the comparisons

Extensions

| SCIENCE | MATHEMATICS |

1. In a learning center, provide objects for students to place in serial order by weight. This additional practice will benefit students who need more experience comparing objects. Or, suggest that students place a set of objects in serial order on the basis of length, width, or height.

| SCIENCE |

2. In a learning center, provide miscellaneous objects and task cards. Here are some ideas for task cards.

   ■ Find something that is heavier (or lighter) than X.

   ■ Which is heavier (or lighter), X or Y?

   ■ Find two objects that are equal to each other. Find one object that is heavier than the two objects together.

   ■ Put four objects from the box in serial order from lightest to heaviest. Now pick out two new objects and determine where they fit in that order.

| SCIENCE |

3. Have students use the beam balance to place the four objects from this lesson in serial order from lightest to heaviest. Ask them to describe any differences or similarities they discover between the results they obtain with the two balances.

| LANGUAGE ARTS |

4. Have students write in their science journals. They could write similes, such as "A ____ is as heavy as a ____," and then illustrate them. Students could write poems or stories about heavy or light objects. They could also write words describing the four objects on sheets of construction paper and use the sheets to create mobiles.

| ART |

5. As a take-home activity, ask students to draw pictures of their family members and place them in serial order by height.

Teacher's Objects

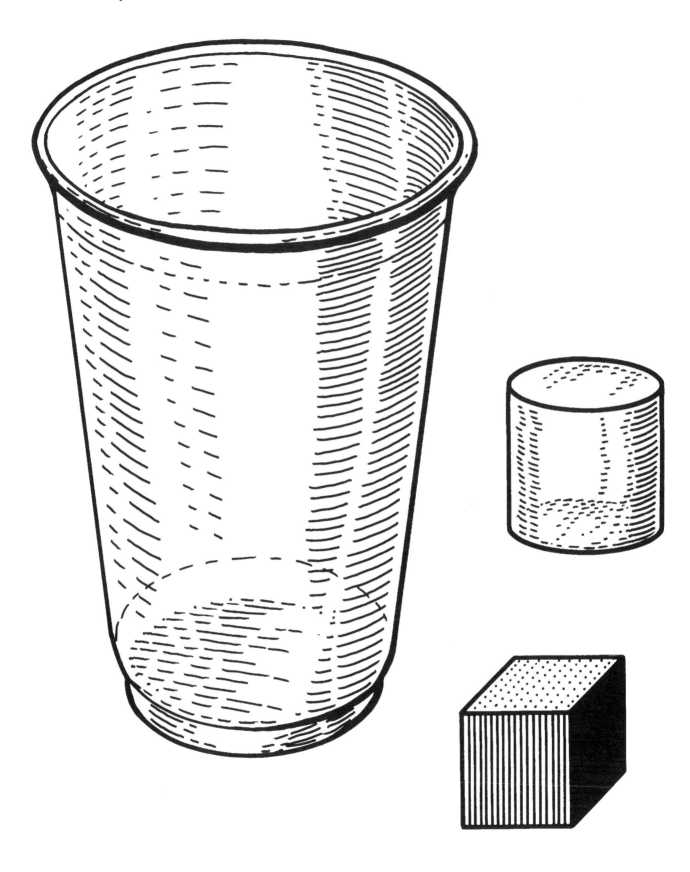

Teacher's Objects, *continued*

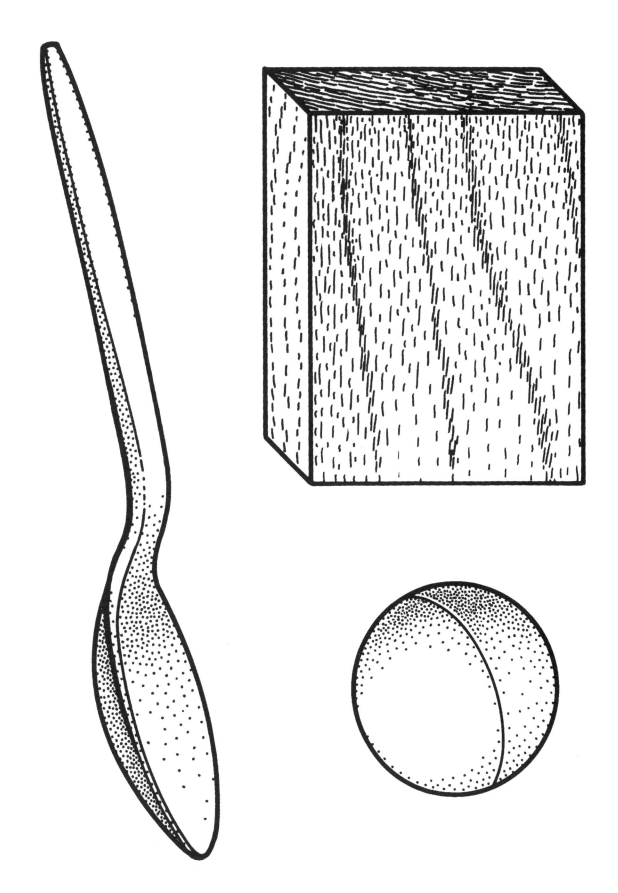

Four Objects

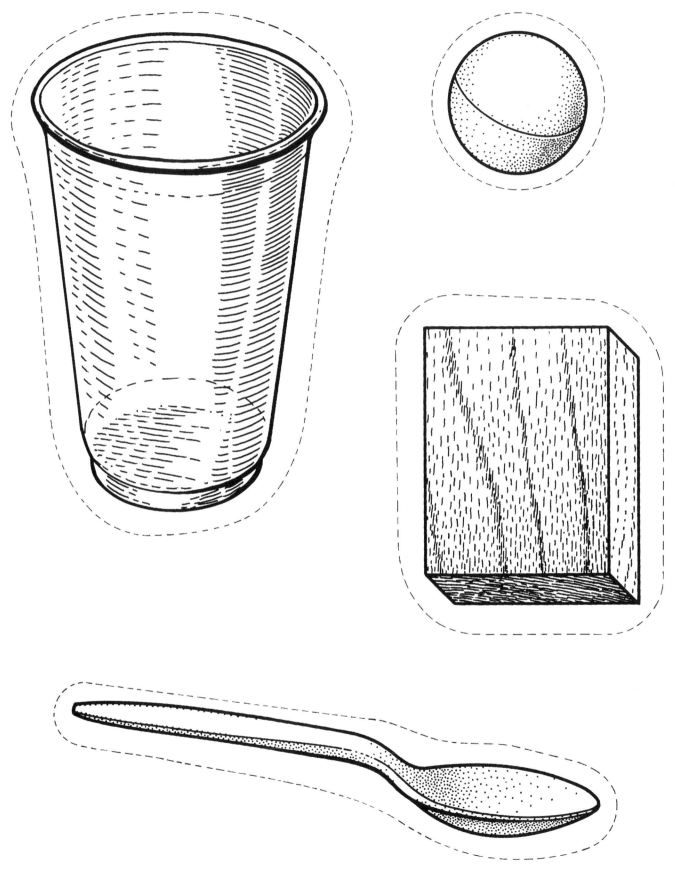

Placing Six Objects in Serial Order

Overview and Objectives

The two main activities in this lesson—placing six objects in serial order and recording this order on paper—challenge students to expand and refine their comparison-making strategies. Students determine where to place two new objects in the serial order of the original four objects from Lesson 8. In the next lesson, they will explore another strategy for comparing objects—weighing.

- Students predict where two new objects will fit in the serial order of four objects established in Lesson 8.

- Students use the equal-arm balance to place six objects in serial order.

- Students record and discuss the serial order of the six objects.

Background

All the issues discussed in the **Background** of Lesson 8 are applicable to this lesson, and you may want to review that section before beginning Lesson 9. The **Assessment** section in Lesson 6 provides suggestions for evaluating specific behaviors you may observe during your students' activities.

Materials

For each student
- 1 pair of scissors
- 1 strip of newsprint with four cutouts attached in serial order (from Lesson 8)

For every two students
- 2 copies of the blackline master **Two New Objects**
- 1 assembled equal-arm balance
- 1 piece of clay
- 1 plastic cup, 296 ml (10 oz)
- 1 Ping-Pong ball
- 1 plastic spoon
- 1 wood block
- 1 metal cube
- 1 acrylic cylinder
- 1 square of Plasti-Tak™ adhesive

For the class

   1   set of six cutouts (from the blackline master **Teacher's Objects** in Lesson 8)

  30   sheets of writing paper

   1   sheet of newsprint

   1   marker

       Plasti-Tak™ adhesive or masking tape

   6   magnets (optional)

Preparation

1. Make enough copies of the blackline master **Two New Objects,** pg. 87, so that each student has a picture of both objects.

2. Make sure you have the cutouts of the acrylic cylinder and the metal cube, which are found on the blackline master **Teacher's Objects,** on pg. 78 in Lesson 8, and the four cutouts that you used in Lesson 8.

3. On the sheet of newsprint, write the title "From Lightest to Heaviest."

4. Assemble the materials in the distribution center. Put the cylinders, metal cubes, writing paper, and the students' newsprint strips in a separate place. You will distribute them during the lesson.

Procedure

1. Distribute the students' strips of newsprint from Lesson 8 and give each child a sheet of writing paper. Then hold up the metal cube and the acrylic cylinder. Let students know that they will add these two objects to their strips and create a new serial order.

2. Distribute the cubes and cylinders. Ask students to feel how heavy or light each object is. Ask them to predict where each will fit in their existing serial order of four objects and to record their predictions on the writing paper.

3. Have students collect the equal-arm balances, a piece of clay, and the four objects from the distribution center.

4. Give students a few moments to equilibrate their equal-arm balances. Then challenge them to devise a strategy to place the six objects in serial order.

Figure 9-1

Comparing the six objects

5. As students complete this activity, have them place the six objects on their desks, from left to right, in the serial order they have determined.

6. Ask students to return the equal-arm balances and clay to the distribution center. Have them pick up the scissors, the blackline master **Two New Objects,** and Plasti-Tak™ adhesive.

7. Have students cut out the pictures of the metal cube and the acrylic cylinder and attach them to their strips in a way that shows the serial order of all six objects.

8. Have students return all materials except the strips to the distribution center.

Figure 9-2

Placing the six objects in serial order

Final Activities

1. Invite students to discuss how their predictions about the serial order of the six objects compared with the results they obtained using the equal-arm balance. On the chart "From Lightest to Heaviest," place your six cutouts in the order that students propose. Write the binary symbols between the objects to show their relationships, as illustrated in Figure 9-3. Have students add the symbols to their strips.

2. Have students discuss the strategies they used to compare the six objects. Students also may want to discuss any changes they made in the order of the original four objects on the basis of the discoveries they made in this lesson.

3. Collect the students' strips and save them for use in the next two lessons.

Figure 9-3

*Recording
students' results*

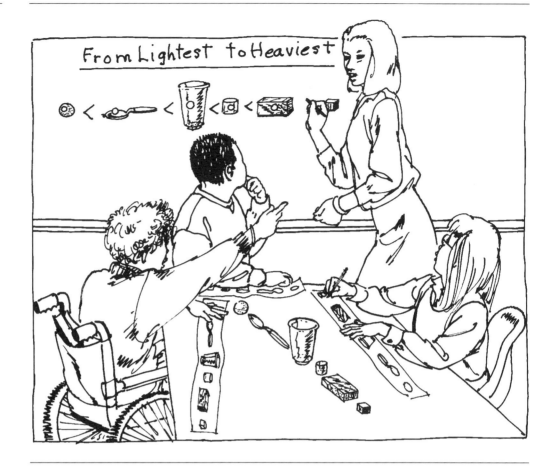

Extensions

LANGUAGE ARTS

1. Have students brainstorm responses to the following question: Why do you think it might be important to know how to put things in serial order? Have students work together in small groups to write about their ideas.

SCIENCE

2. In a learning center, provide objects for students to put in serial order. Encourage them to compare more than six objects.

MATHEMATICS

3. Encourage students to look for other objects at school or home whose shapes are similar to those of the six objects they have been comparing. Have them predict the weight of each of the objects and then draw them in serial order from lightest to heaviest.

Assessment

In Lessons 6 to 9, students have explored how the equal-arm balance works and how they can use it to compare objects. The guidelines provided on pgs. 61–62 in Lesson 6 will help you assess students' growth.

Two New Objects

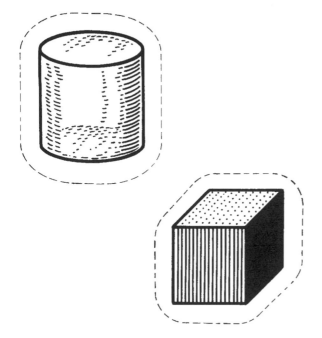

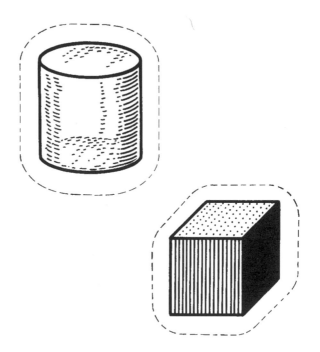

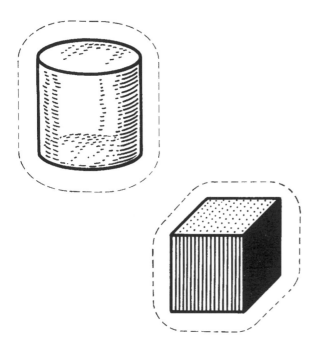

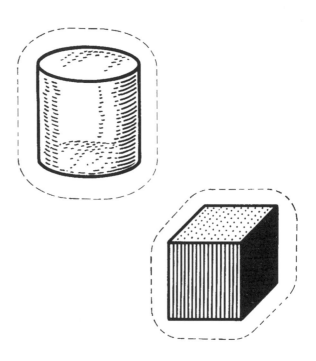

LESSON 10   Balancing with Unifix Cubes™

Overview and Objectives

This lesson shifts the focus of activity to using the equal-arm balance as a tool for weighing objects. Students discover that weighing is the process of balancing an object against a certain number of standard units. As they enter their findings on a class data table, students discuss reasons for the varied results that their classmates have obtained. They discover how to determine a single number that represents the weight recorded by most of the class members for each object. In Lesson 11, students will present their discoveries about weighing with Unifix Cubes™ in a graph.

- Students use Unifix Cubes™ to balance objects on the equal-arm balance.

- Students record their results on individual record sheets and a class data table.

- Students compare and discuss the information on the class data table.

- Students discuss the relationship between balancing and weighing.

Background

In Lessons 6 to 9, students compared objects by observing the movement of the pails of the equal-arm balance. In this lesson, they discover that they can weigh an object by determining how many Unifix Cubes™ are needed to balance it. This activity is referred to as "balancing" until the end of the lesson; once students have had the opportunity to discover the connection between balancing and weighing, the term "weighing" is introduced.

When students weigh the objects, they will probably obtain different results. One reason for these discrepancies is that similar objects may differ in weight; for example, no two wood blocks weigh exactly the same. You will need to discuss this with your students.

Materials

For each student
  1 copy of **Record Sheet 10-A: Balancing with Unifix Cubes**™

For every two students
  1 assembled equal-arm balance
  1 piece of clay
  1 set of six objects—Ping-Pong ball, plastic spoon, plastic cup, wood block, acrylic cylinder, and metal cube
 30 Unifix Cubes™
  6 Post-it™ notes, 76 mm (3 in) square

For the class

　1　sheet of newsprint

　1　marker

　1　set of six cutouts (from blackline master **Teacher's Objects,** Lesson 8)
　　　Plasti-Tak™ or masking tape

　6　magnets (optional)

Preparation

1. Make a copy of **Record Sheet 10-A: Balancing with Unifix Cubes**™ (pg. 96) for each student.

2. On a sheet of newsprint, create a data table that you will use to record the weight of the six objects. Figure 10-1 illustrates how to set up this table. Since the table will be used over the next three lessons, you may want to make it on poster board. Note that the title of the right column will change from "Number of Cubes" to "Weight" in Lesson 11.

3. Remove six Post-it™ notes from the pad for every two students.

4. Assemble all the materials except the Post-it™ notes in the distribution center.

Figure 10-1

Class data table

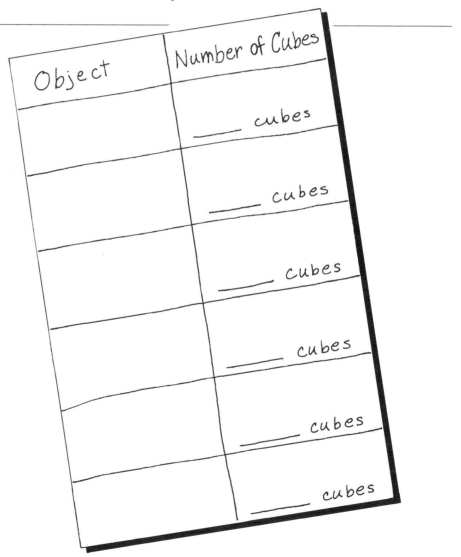

Procedure

1. Briefly review with students the sequence of their activities during the past nine lessons. Highlight the progression they have made: balancing an object on a fulcrum (the butterfly activity), achieving balance by varying weight and the position of weight in relation to the position of the fulcrum (the beam balance and the mobile), balancing objects on the equal-arm balance, and using the equal-arm balance to compare objects and arrange them in serial order from lightest to heaviest.

2. Let students know that in this lesson they will balance each object with Unifix Cubes™.

3. Distribute a copy of **Record Sheet 10-A: Balancing with Unifix Cubes**™ to each student. Ask students to write the names of the six objects in the left column from lightest (top) to heaviest (bottom). Figure 10-2 shows an example of this serial order.

Figure 10-2

Preparing the record sheet

4. Place an object in one pail of an equal-arm balance. Ask students to discuss how they could use the Unifix Cubes™ to balance the cross beam. Let students know that they will now have an opportunity to explore some of these strategies.

5. Ask students to collect their materials from the distribution center and to begin the activity. Make sure they equilibrate the equal-arm balance before they start. Remind them to record their results on the record sheet.

6. After students complete the activity, have them return all materials to the distribution center.

Figure 10-3

*Balancing with
Unifix Cubes™*

Final Activities

1. Display the class data table. Using your six cutouts, ask students to help you place the objects in serial order from top to bottom, lightest to heaviest. Adhere the cutouts to the data table with magnets, folded masking tape, or Plasti-Tak™.

2. Distribute six Post-it™ notes to every two students. Ask them to write on these notes the number of Unifix Cubes™ they needed to balance each object. Then have partners share the task of adhering the notes on the appropriate spot on the data table.

3. Review the results recorded on the data table. If students reported different numbers of Unifix Cubes™ for an object, discuss the possible reasons for the variations. Students may suggest some of the following reasons:

   ■ The equal-arm balances were not all level before beginning.

   ■ Some students may have miscounted the number of Unifix Cubes™ in the pail.

   ■ Objects may differ in weight, even though they look quite similar.

   ■ An object may balance between two numbers of Unifix Cubes™. In this case, some students may have used the lower number, while others used the higher number.

4. If any students' results are dramatically different from those of a majority of their classmates, you may want them to check their results by balancing the object again.

   Note: To prevent students from feeling as though their results were "wrong," recall some of the ideas they discussed for finding different numbers. Assure them that the reasons for the differences can be valid.

Figure 10-4

Posting results on
the class data table

5. Even after students have rechecked their results and some have changed
their numbers, it is likely that more than one number will still be recorded
for each object. Ask students how they might decide on a single number of
Unifix Cubes™ for each object. If students do not bring it up themselves, let
them know that one way is to see which number is recorded most often.

6. Have the students help you tally the numbers recorded in each column to find
the number that occurs most frequently for each object. Once you have found
one number for each object, remove the Post-it™ notes and write that number
in the column. Figure 10-5 is an example of the results you might obtain.
Your numbers may be different, depending on your students' actual findings.

Figure 10-5

Sample of a completed class data table

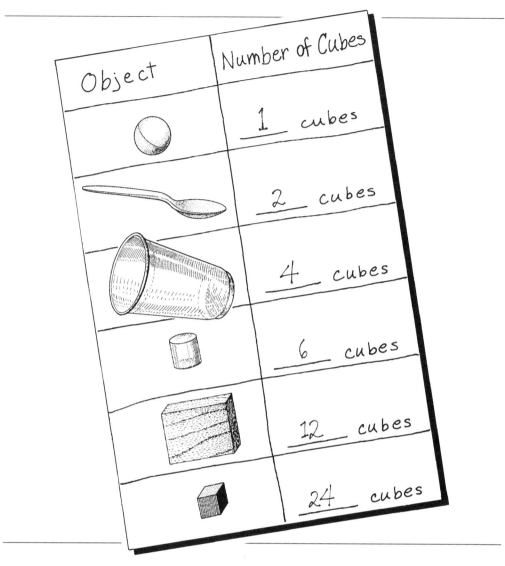

Object	Number of Cubes
(ball)	_1_ cubes
(spoon)	_2_ cubes
(cup)	_4_ cubes
(cylinder)	_6_ cubes
(wood block)	_12_ cubes
(cube)	_24_ cubes

7. Introduce the word "weighing." Ask students to describe what they think it means. Encourage them to discuss why the activity they have done in this lesson can be called weighing.

Extensions

SCIENCE   MATHEMATICS

1. In a learning center, challenge students to solve problems using the equal-arm balance, Unifix Cubes™, and miscellaneous objects. Ideas for task cards include the following:

   ■ Find something that weighs more than six Unifix Cubes™.

   ■ Find something that weighs two Unifix Cubes™.

   ■ Find something that weighs less than the wood block.

LANGUAGE ARTS

2. Have students list places where they have seen things or people being weighed. Add these ideas to the "Ways We Balance and Weigh" chart. Have students illustrate their ideas or cut out pictures from magazines. Bind the illustrations and pictures into a class book or use them to create a bulletin board.

LANGUAGE ARTS

3. In their science journals, have students write about weighing. These sentence starters may help guide their writing.

   ■ The heaviest object I ever lifted was _____.

   ■ I think a _____ is lighter than a _____ because _____.

   ■ Weight means _____.

Assessment

The activities in Lessons 10 and 11 provide students with the opportunity to use the equal-arm balance to weigh objects. The following guidelines are suggested as ways to help you assess your students during these lessons.

Lesson 10

■ What strategies do students apply to balance each object with Unifix Cubes™?

■ What ideas do students suggest to explain any variations in results?

Lesson 11

Data Table

■ How do students use the information on the data table to answer questions?

Bar Graphs

■ Do students place the six objects in serial order on the graph?

■ How do students represent the information on the data table in their graphs?

■ Do the students' titles relate to the information on the graph?

■ If students have entered any misrepresentations on their graphs, how do they correct them?

Comparing the Serial Order Strip with the Bar Graph

■ Do students recognize any differences between the serial order of the six objects on their strips and the order on the graph? How do they explain these differences?

■ Listen for students' ideas about observing the movement of the pails as a way of comparing objects versus quantifying weight with a standard unit as a means of comparing the objects. Do students suggest why one strategy might be more effective than the other?

Record Sheet 10-A

Name: _____

Date: _____

Balancing with Unifix Cubes™

Object	Number of Cubes
	_____ cubes
	_____ cubes
	_____ cubes
	_____ cubes
	_____ cubes
	_____ cubes

Graphing the Weights of the Objects

Overview and Objectives

In this lesson, students examine the advantages and disadvantages of observing the movement of the pails of the equal-arm balance versus weighing as strategies for placing six objects in serial order. They are challenged to design bar graphs that show the weight of each of the objects. Comparing their graphs with the serial order strips from Lesson 9 helps them draw conclusions concerning which strategy provides more information. A reading selection at the end of the lesson, "Weighing Animals at the Zoo," provides unusual examples of an everyday use of weighing.

- Students review the information on the data table from Lesson 10.

- Students make bar graphs that show the weights of the six objects.

- Students compare their bar graphs with their serial order strips and discuss the similarities and differences between them.

- Students read about how animals are weighed at the zoo.

Background

In this lesson, students have an opportunity to make their own bar graphs and to decide how to present data about the weights of the six objects they studied in Lesson 10. This experience can help them better understand the purpose of bar graphs, how to design them, and how to interpret the information they contain.

Students may need some guidance about the materials they will use to make their graphs; however, instructions about how to design the graphs should remain open-ended. This will encourage students to make their own decisions about how to present their information. It will also give you an opportunity to evaluate your students' ability to design bar graphs and to transfer information to them. Figure 11-1 illustrates some graphs made by second-grade students.

Materials

For each student

- 1 pair of scissors
- 1 copy of the blackline master **Objects for the Graph**
- 1 copy of the blackline master **The Cube Towers**
- 1 serial order strip (from Lesson 9)
- 1 copy of "Weighing Animals at the Zoo"
    Glue, tape, or paste
    Crayons (optional)

Figure 11-1

*Five students'
bar graphs*

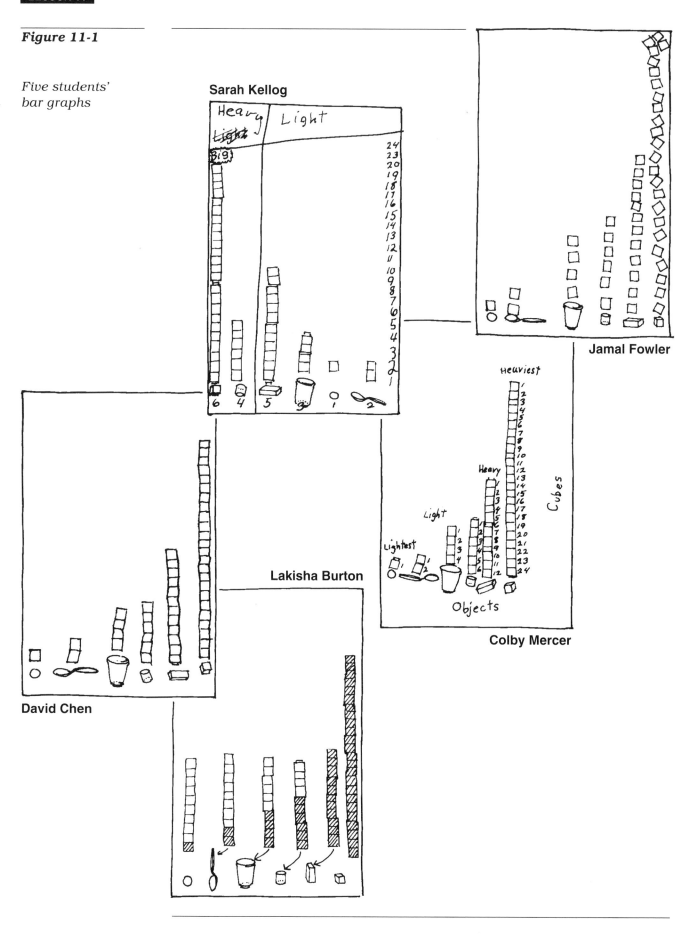

Sarah Kellog

Jamal Fowler

David Chen

Lakisha Burton

Colby Mercer

For the class

  15   sheets of newsprint, 61 × 92 cm (24 × 36 in)

   1   data table (from Lesson 10)

   1   set of six cutouts (from Lesson 9)

       Plasti-Tak™ or masking tape

   6   magnets (optional)

       "Ways We Balance and Weigh" chart (from Lesson 2)

Preparation

1. Make one copy for each student of the reading selection "Weighing Animals at the Zoo," found on pgs. 105–106.

2. Make one copy for each student of the blackline master **Objects for the Graph,** found on pg. 107, and the blackline master **The Cube Towers,** found on pg. 108. You may want to make extra copies of the cube towers in case students need them to complete their graphs.

3. Cut each of the 15 sheets of newsprint in half along the longer side. Each half-sheet should measure 61 × 46 cm (24 × 18 in).

4. Arrange all materials except the serial order strips in the distribution center.

5. On the data table from Lesson 10, tape a piece of paper over the title "Number of Cubes." Retitle this column "Weight." Hang the data table in a place that is visible to all students. Using tape, magnets, or Plasti-Tak™, arrange the six cutouts in random order in the left column of the table.

   Note: Remember that the weights shown on the data table in this lesson and the others are only examples. The weights on which your students agree may be different.

Procedure

1. To review the results from Lesson 10, ask students to help you rearrange the six objects on the data table in serial order on the basis of weight. Point out that the column titled "Number of Cubes" is now labeled "Weight."

2. Ask students the following questions. Encourage them to use the data table when making comparisons and drawing conclusions.

   ■ How many Unifix Cubes™ does the cup (or any of the other objects) weigh?

   ■ Which object weighs the most Unifix Cubes™? Which object weighs the fewest Unifix Cubes™?

   ■ Do any two objects weigh the same?

   ■ What weighs more, the cylinder or the cup?

   ■ How much heavier is the metal cube than the wood block?

   ■ Does any object weigh almost two times as much as another object?

3. Now let students know that they will make bar graphs to show the information that appears on the data table.

   ■ Show students a half-sheet of newsprint. Let them know they will need to turn it so that the longer side is vertical.

   ■ Now show students the blackline master **Objects for the Graph.** Let them know that they will cut out the objects and place them in serial order, from lightest to heaviest, across the bottom of the newsprint, from left to right.

Figure 11-2

Sample class data table showing the six objects in random order

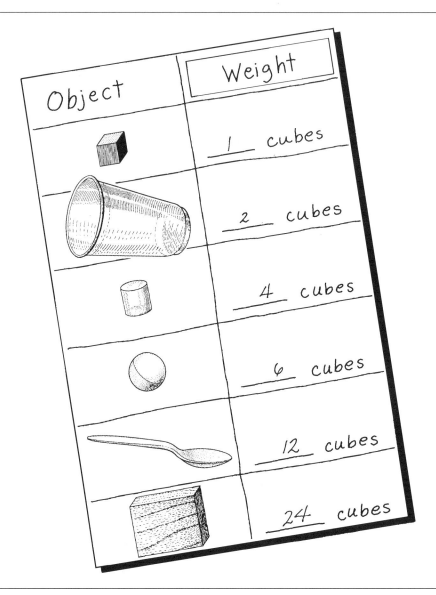

- Finally, show the students the blackline master **The Cube Towers.** Let them know they will first cut out as many cubes as they need. Then they will glue or tape the appropriate number of cubes above each object to show its weight.

4. Ask students to collect their materials and begin making their graphs. Remind them to use the data table as a source of information.

5. As students complete this activity, ask them to decide on a title for the graph and to write the title at the top of the sheet. Make sure students write their names on the bottom of the graph.

6. Have students return their materials to the distribution center. Ask them to keep their graphs at their desks.

Figure 11-3

Arranging the objects in serial order

Final Activities

1. Ask several students to describe their graphs. Encourage other students to ask questions during these presentations. You also might want to revisit the questions in Step 2 of the **Procedure** section on pg. 101. This time, ask students to use their graphs rather than the data table as the source of information.

2. Distribute the serial order strips from Lesson 9. Ask students to compare the information on their strips with that on their graph. The following questions may help guide this discussion:

   ■ What information is the same on both the strip and the graph? What information is different?

   ■ Is the serial order of the six objects the same on both the graph and the strip? If some students find different serial orders, have the class discuss reasons for these variations.

   ■ Which gives you more information about the six objects, the strip or the graph? Why?

   ■ The objects on the strip were arranged on the basis of comparing the six objects with one another by observing the movement of the pails, while the graph was made as a result of weighing the objects. Do you think one strategy is more helpful than the other? Why?

3. Draw students' attention to the "Ways We Balance and Weigh" chart. Introduce the idea that weighing enables you to quantify weight. For example, a bathroom scale doesn't tell you that you are light or heavy; it tells you how much you weigh. Ask students to discuss this idea and to think of other places where they have seen things weighed. Add their ideas to the chart.

4. Distribute copies of "Weighing Animals at the Zoo." Let students know this story is based on an interview with Shawn Mallan, a zookeeper at the Smithsonian Institution's National Zoological Park in Washington, D.C. Read the story to the class or have students read it aloud in pairs or silently to themselves. Then ask students to discuss the following questions:

   ■ How might a zookeeper weigh other animals?

   ■ How much do you think a hippopotamus weighs? Do you think it weighs more or less than an elephant? How could you find out?

Extensions

LANGUAGE ARTS

1. To supplement the reading selection, invite students to write about and illustrate their ideas for how zookeepers might weigh other animals. If there is a zoo or nature center in your area, plan a class visit so that students can actually see animals being weighed. After the visit, create a class book.

SCIENCE

2. Assemble materials to compare and weigh in a learning center. Then create task cards. Here are some examples of ideas for task cards.

   ■ I weigh nine Unifix Cubes™. What am I?

   ■ I am heavier than 6 Unifix Cubes™ but lighter than 10. What am I?

   ■ I weigh the same as four wood blocks. What am I?

MATHEMATICS

3. Have students make bar graphs or line plots that show class information such as hair color, eye color, height, number of pets, favorite foods, or shoe styles. Or, have them design questions about a topic and interview students in other classes and then make a bar graph to convey their results.

Reading Selection

Weighing Animals at the Zoo

How would you weigh an animal as big as an elephant or as small as a mouse? The elephant wouldn't fit in the pails of your equal-arm balance. And what if the mouse jumped out before you could weigh it?

Zookeepers have ways to solve these problems. For one thing, all of their scales are run by computers. This means that they can get the weights quickly. When zookeepers are working with large animals, like elephants, this is very important.

"We use two scales to weigh elephants," explains Shawn Mallan, a zookeeper at the National Zoo. "The elephant puts its right front leg on one scale and its left rear leg on the second scale. It keeps the other two legs in the air. While the trainer tends to the elephant, we read its weight off the scale. It takes only a few seconds. One elephant weighs about as much as 100 second-grade students. That's about 6,000 to 9,000 pounds!"

Some animals, such as sea lions, can be trained to walk right onto the scale. The zookeepers place tiny animals, such as mice, in cloth bags and weigh them on smaller scales.

Of course, not all animals can be trained to cooperate. It's hard to figure out a way to get a giraffe or an ostrich to walk onto a scale.

How do you think zookeepers weigh these animals? Share your ideas with your partner.

Objects for the Graph

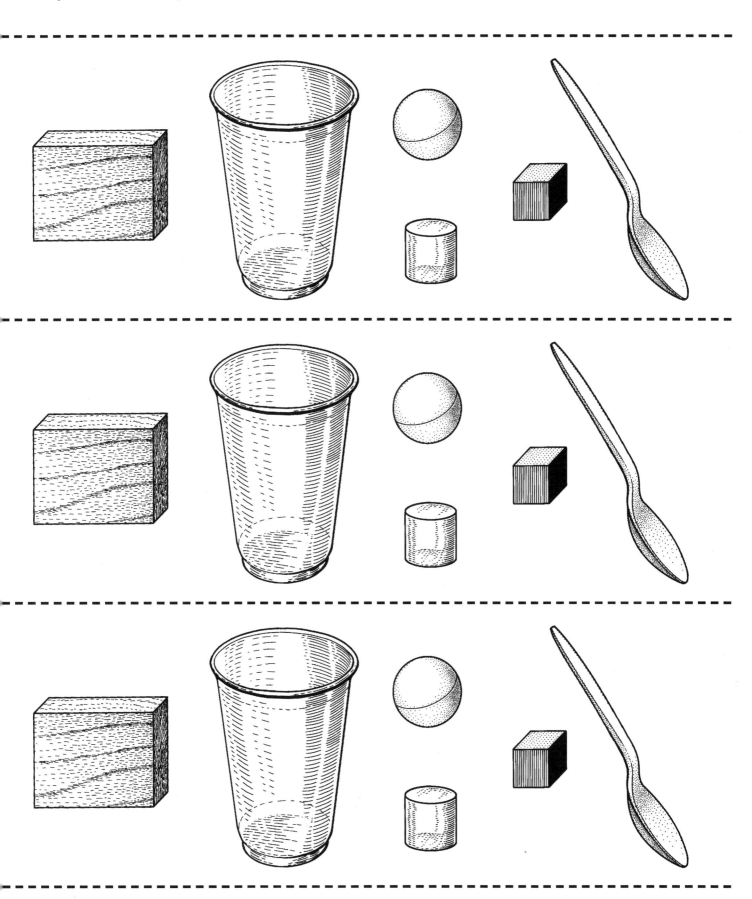

The Cube Towers

Describing the Four Foods

Overview and Objectives

Lesson 12 is the first of a sequence of four lessons in which students apply their comparing and weighing skills to solve problems that involve four foods of varying weights, shapes, and sizes. These foods are sunflower seeds, round oat cereal, macaroni, and split peas. Students begin their activities by using their observing and recording skills to describe the properties of the four foods. Later, they will apply their observations to help explain why equal cupfuls of the four foods have different weights.

- Students observe and describe the properties of four different foods.

- Students record their descriptions of the four foods.

- Students share their observations of the foods and create a class chart.

- Students compare and contrast their observations of the foods.

Background

As students experiment with the four foods in Lessons 12 through 15, they will make two important observations. The first is that equal cupfuls of the four foods weigh different amounts; the second, that equal weights of the foods occupy different amounts of space. Students will begin by using the equal-arm balance to place cupfuls of the four foods in serial order from lightest to heaviest. Then they will reverse the established procedure for weighing—instead of determining how many Unifix Cubes™ they need to balance a certain amount of each food, they will determine how much of each food is required to balance a constant number of Unifix Cubes™.

Before undertaking these investigations, students have the opportunity to explore the four foods. Their observations focus on four properties—color, shape, size, and texture. In upcoming lessons, students will find out that some of these properties affect the amount of space the foods occupy, while others do not.

Materials

For each student
- 1   copy of **Record Sheet 12-A: Describing the Foods**
- 1   piece of each of the four foods—sunflower seeds, round oat cereal, macaroni, and split peas
- 1   small plastic cup, 74 ml (2½ oz)

For the class

    1   set of six objects (from Lesson 9)

    1   sheet of newsprint

    1   marker

Preparation

1. Make one copy for each student of **Record Sheet 12-A: Describing the Foods,** on pg. 115.

2. Place one piece of each of the four foods in the 30 plastic cups.

3. On the sheet of newsprint, write the title "Describing the Foods." Figure 12-1 illustrates how to make this chart.

Figure 12-1

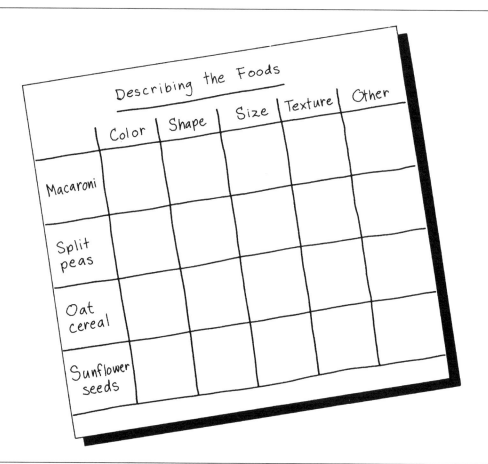

Procedure

1. Hold up the six objects that students worked with earlier in the unit and ask them to discuss why the objects weigh different amounts. They may suggest, for example, that weight is related to the object's size or to what it is made of. They may also suggest that weight depends on what is inside the object; for example, the Ping-Pong ball is full of air, but the wooden block is solid.

2. Let students know that in the next few lessons they will compare and weigh foods. Today, they will begin by observing and describing one piece of each of the foods.

Safety Tip

The sunflower seeds have not been processed for human consumption and may contain small rocks or twigs. Discuss with students the importance of not using the sense of taste in science class. You will want to mention that the other senses can provide equally important information.

3. Distribute a cup containing one piece of each of the four foods and a copy of **Record Sheet 12-A: Describing the Foods** to each student. Depending on your students' experience with observing an object and describing its properties, you may need to review the four properties—color, shape, size, and texture—on the record sheet with them.

4. Ask the students to observe the foods and to record their descriptions of them.

Figure 12-2

Exploring the four foods

Final Activities

1. Ask each student to share one description of one of the foods with the class. Record each observation on the chart entitled "Describing the Foods." Write any observations that do not fit with the four properties in the column labeled "Other."

2. When the chart is complete, ask students to compare the foods. The following questions may help guide this discussion:

    ■ Which food is biggest?

    ■ Which food is smallest?

    ■ Which foods are alike? How are they alike?

■ Which foods are different? How are they different?

■ Which food do you think is heaviest? Lightest?

3. Collect the cups and food. Leave the chart on display for use in the next three lessons.

Extensions

┌─────────────┐
│ **SCIENCE** │
└─────────────┘

1. Give students a variety of objects to observe, describe, and sort by specific properties. Encourage them to group the items more than once, using a different property each time.

┌──────────────────┐
│ **LANGUAGE ARTS** │
└──────────────────┘

2. Have students write in their science journals about the questions discussed in Step 2 of the **Final Activities.**

Assessment

In Lessons 12 to 15, students will observe that equal cupfuls of food weigh different amounts and that equal weights of the foods occupy different amounts of space. The guidelines suggested here can help you assess your students' understanding as they progress through these lessons.

Lessons 12, 13, and 14

■ What ideas do students suggest to explain why the six objects weigh different amounts? Are the ideas based on their observations of and experiences with the objects?

■ Do students articulate their understanding that large objects are not always heavier than small ones?

■ What strategies do students apply to compare and weigh the cupfuls of food and arrange them in serial order?

■ Do students suggest that the weight of each cupful is affected by the shape of the food and how closely the pieces pack together?

■ What reasons do students suggest for the various weights recorded on the line plots? Do they recognize that the reasons for the range of results are valid?

Lesson 15

■ Are students able to weigh 10 Unifix Cubes™ of each food? Does reversing the weighing procedure confuse some students?

■ How do students describe the relationship between the size of the food, its weight, and amount of space it occupies? For example, do they discuss that the smallest food takes up the least space but is also the heaviest food?

■ How do students apply their observations from the previous lessons to help them explain why equal weights of food take up different amounts of space?

■ How do students summarize and consolidate their observations during the **Final Activities?**

Record Sheet 12-A

Name: -

Date: -

Describing the Foods

Food	Color	Shape	Size	Texture
Macaroni				
Split peas				
Oat cereal				
Sunflower seeds				

Comparing Cupfuls of Food

Overview and Objectives

Students have now observed and described the properties of the four foods. In this lesson, they apply their observations to help explain why equal cupfuls of the foods have different weights. Using the equal-arm balance, students compare cupfuls of the foods and place them in serial order from lightest to heaviest. In Lesson 14, students will use Unifix Cubes™ to determine the weight of each cupful.

- Students predict a serial order for a cupful of each of the four foods, from lightest to heaviest.

- Students compare the weights of the four cupfuls of food.

- Students discuss the results of their comparisons.

Background

? predict

Today, students discover that equal cupfuls of each of the four foods have different weights. The weights are different for two reasons: each food has a different density, and each packs differently into the cup. For example, a cupful of split peas is heavier than a cupful of round oat cereal not only because each split pea is denser than each piece of oat cereal but also because the split peas pack more closely together than the pieces of cereal. The way the foods pack is related to one of their observable properties—shape.

Your students will probably observe that the number of split peas in the cup is greater than the number of pieces of round oat cereal. They may use this observation to explain why the cupful of split peas weighs more. Let them know that the number of pieces does not explain why one cupful is heavier than another. For example, they could cut each piece of cereal in half. They would have twice as many pieces, but the weight of the cereal would still be the same. Even if your students do not raise this point, it is important to help them understand that a greater number of objects does not necessarily weigh more than a smaller number of objects.

Materials

For each student
    1   copy of **Record Sheet 13-A: Comparing Cupfuls of Food**

For every two students
    1   assembled equal-arm balance
    1   piece of clay
    4   small plastic cups, 74 ml (2½ oz)

Figure 13-1

Distribution center

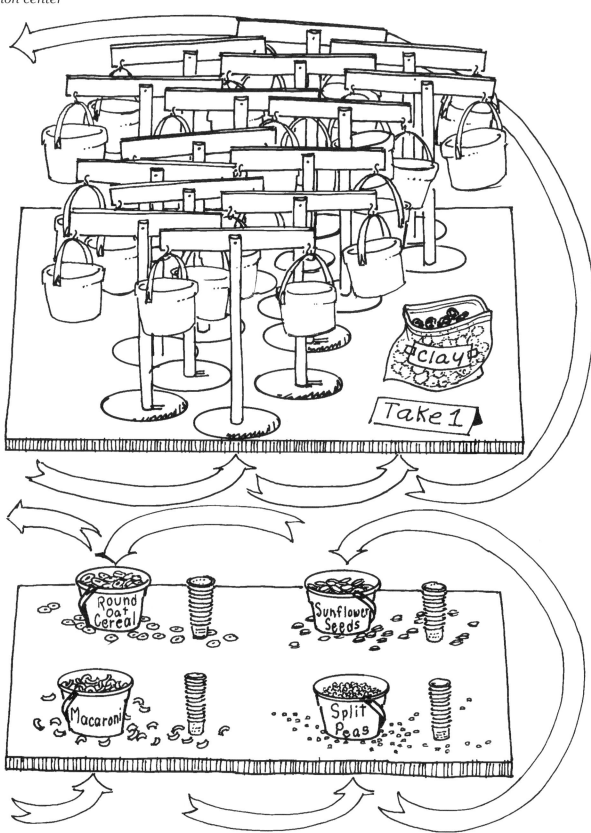

For the class
1 sheet of newsprint
1 marker
1 plastic pail of round oat cereal, 340 g (12 oz)
1 plastic pail of macaroni, 680 g (1½ lb)
1 plastic pail of sunflower seeds, 450 g (1 lb)
1 plastic pail of split peas, 1.3 kg (2½ lb)
   "Describing the Foods" chart (from Lesson 12)

Preparation

1. Make one copy of **Record Sheet 13-A: Comparing Cupfuls of Food,** pg. 122, for each student.

2. Assemble the materials in the distribution center. Students will pick up one small plastic cupful of food from each of the four pails. Arrange the pails so that students can move easily around the table. One way to arrange the distribution center is shown in Figure 13-1.

3. On the sheet of newsprint, write the title "Why Cupfuls of Food Are Lighter and Heavier."

4. Make sure that "Describing the Foods," the chart from Lesson 12, is posted in a visible location.

Procedure

1. Let students know that instead of looking at one piece of each of the foods, as they did in the last lesson, they will now have a cupful of each food. They will compare the four cupfuls and arrange them in serial order from lightest to heaviest.

2. Show students four empty cups and ask them to describe how they are alike. Help the students focus on the fact that the cups are identical in size and shape.

3. Now review the importance of fair comparisons. Let students know that using identical cups will help make their comparisons fair. Explain that it is also important to fill the cups equally. In order to make fair comparisons, the contents should be level with the top of the cup. Students can do this by over-filling the cup and then sliding a finger across the top to remove excess food (see Figure 13-2).

4. Have each pair of students get one cupful of food from each of the four pails in the distribution center. Students can divide this task so that each partner picks up two cupfuls.

5. Ask students to predict a serial order for the foods, from lightest to heaviest.

6. Distribute a copy of **Record Sheet 13-A: Comparing Cupfuls of Food** to each student. Have them record their predictions.

7. Now have students collect the equal-arm balances and clay. After they have equilibrated the balances, have them begin comparing the cupfuls of food. Remind them to write their results on the record sheets.

8. As students complete the activity, ask them to return all materials to the distribution center and to empty each cupful into the appropriate pail. Have them clean up any food that has dropped near their work space. They should keep their record sheets at their desks.

Figure 13-2

Leveling a cupful of food

Final Activities

1. Ask students to compare their predictions with their results. How were they the same? How did they differ?

2. Ask students to discuss why they think a cupful of one food may weigh more (or less) than a cupful of another food. Encourage them to refer to the descriptions of the foods that appear on the class chart entitled "Describing the Foods."

3. Record students' thoughts on the new chart titled "Why Cupfuls of Food Are Heavier and Lighter." The following statements are examples of observations your students may make:

   ■ There is a lot of air inside the macaroni, and air is light.

   ■ The oat cereal is lighter because it is full of holes and air.

   ■ The bigger foods take up more room in the cup, so you cannot put as many pieces in.

   ■ A lot of split peas can be put into one cup because they fit together very closely. The peas are also smaller than the other foods.

4. Keep the charts used in Steps 2 and 3 on display for the next two lessons.

Extensions

MATHEMATICS

1. Have students make graphs comparing the quantity of food found in each cup. They can do this by counting the pieces of food in each cupful and then gluing the pieces to a long strip of paper. Challenge them to find a way to organize the pieces of food into groups of 10.

Figure 13-3

Comparing cupfuls of food with the equal-arm balance

SCIENCE

2. Set up a learning center and stock it with containers of various sizes and water or sand. Have students experiment with the capacity of the containers.

SCIENCE

3. Bring in cans of food that are identical in size and shape but different in weight. Remove the labels. Have students compare the weights of the cans and then place them in serial order from lightest to heaviest. Encourage students to guess what is in each can.

Record Sheet 13-A

Name: _____

Date: _____

Comparing Cupfuls of Food

Write the name of the food on the line below each cup.

1. My predictions.

Lightest   Heaviest

_____ _____ _____ _____

2. What I discovered.

Lightest   Heaviest

_____ _____ _____ _____

Weighing Cupfuls of Food

Overview and Objectives

Through comparisons with the equal-arm balance and class discussion, students have discovered that equal-sized cupfuls of different foods may not weigh the same. In this lesson, they apply the skills acquired during previous lessons to weigh a cupful of each of the four foods. They are then introduced to a new method of recording their findings, a class line plot. The line plot enables students to determine the weight obtained by the most members of the class for each food.

- Students weigh a cupful of each of the four foods.

- Students record the weight of a cupful of each food on a class line plot.

- Students identify the weight obtained by the most members of the class for each cupful of food.

Background

Students continue to gain information about the four cupfuls of food as they weigh them with Unifix Cubes™. They are also introduced to a new type of graph, a line plot. A line plot is an effective way to consolidate and display data. Students will make four line plots, one for each food. These graphs will clearly show both the range of weights for each cupful of food and the **mode weight,** which is the weight obtained by more members of the class than any other weight.

To create the class line plots, each pair of students will attach a colored stick-on circle to a number line that shows the weight they obtained for each cupful. A completed class line plot for macaroni is illustrated in Figure 14-1, which shows a mode weight of 17 Unifix Cubes™.

Figure 14-1

Class line plot for macaroni

Macaroni

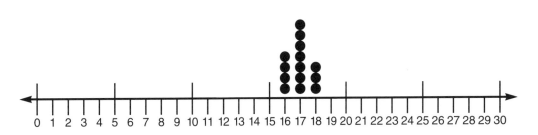

Number of Cubes

Materials

For each student

1 copy of **Record Sheet 14-A: Weighing Cupfuls of Food**

For every two students

1 assembled equal-arm balance
1 piece of clay
4 small plastic cups, 74 ml (2½ oz)
30 Unifix Cubes™
4 colored stick-on circles (one each of red, green, orange, and blue)

For the class

4 sheets of newsprint
4 colored markers (one each of red, green, orange, and blue)
1 pair of scissors
1 plastic pail of round oat cereal, 340 g (12 oz)
1 plastic pail of macaroni, 680 g (1½ lb)
1 plastic pail of sunflower seeds, 450 g (1 lb)
1 plastic pail of split peas, 1.3 kg (2½ lb)

Preparation

1. Make one copy of **Record Sheet 14-A: Weighing Cupfuls of Food,** on pg. 130, for each student.

2. On each of four sheets of newsprint, draw a number line from 0 to 30. Use a different-colored marker for each one. Beneath each number line, write "Number of Cubes." Label each chart with the name of one of the four foods. Figure 14-2 illustrates a number line for macaroni.

3. Cut up the sheets of stick-on circles so that students can easily pick up one circle of each color. Place the circles, the four pails of food, the Unifix Cubes™, and the plastic cups in the distribution center.

Figure 14-2

Number line for macaroni

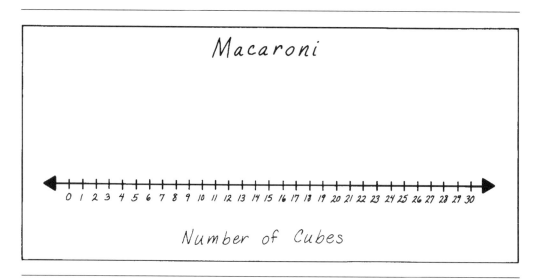

Procedure

1. Ask students to review what they discovered in the last lesson. Have them describe the serial order that they established for the cupfuls of food.

2. Let students know that now they will weigh a cupful of each food and create class graphs to show their results.

3. Distribute a copy of **Record Sheet 14-A: Weighing Cupfuls of Food** to each student.

4. Ask students to collect their materials from the distribution center. As a way of reminding students to level the cups as they collect the food, you could ask a few students to demonstrate or review the procedure for leveling.

5. Have students begin to weigh each cupful of food. Ask them to record their results on the record sheet.

    Note: Figure 14-3 shows the approximate weight of a cupful of each of the four foods. The weights that your students obtain will probably be slightly different.

Figure 14-3

Approximate Weight of a Cupful of Each Food

Food	Approximate Weight
Oat Cereal	4 cubes
Sunflower seeds	12 cubes
Macaroni	17 cubes
Split Peas	25 cubes

Figure 14-4

Weighing cupfuls of food

6. When students finish weighing the foods, explain how they will adhere the stick-on circles to the number lines. Have pairs of students attach one circle (the color should match the number line) above the appropriate number to show the weight of each cupful.

    Note: As they place their stickers on the line plots, some students may discover that their results vary a great deal from those of their classmates. Some teachers have found that this prompts students to voluntarily recheck their results. You may want to provide extra time to allow students to confirm their results.

7. Have students return all materials to the distribution center. Ask them to empty the foods into the appropriate pails and to clean up any food that has dropped near their work space.

Final Activities

1. Ask students to use the line plots to determine the weight obtained by the most students for each cupful of food. The following questions may help guide a discussion:

   ■ What is the range of weights recorded for the sunflower seeds (or any of the other foods)?

   ■ What weight is recorded most often?

   ■ What weight shows the result found by the most students?

2. Have students analyze the information they obtained in this lesson by asking some of the following questions:

   ■ Which cupful of food weighs the most? The least?

   ■ Look at the serial order of the cupfuls. Is it the same as it was in Lesson 13? Did weighing the cupfuls provide more information to help you place them in serial order?

   ■ Think about only one piece of each food. Which is biggest? Smallest?

   ■ Is a cupful of the biggest food the heaviest?

   ■ Is a cupful of the smallest food the lightest?

3. Challenge students to carry their observations about weight a step further by asking the following questions:

   ■ Were you weighing anything other than foods in this lesson? What?

   ■ How could you find out how much the cup weighs?

4. Leave the line plots on display. Students will refer to them in Lesson 15.

Extensions

MATHEMATICS

1. Encourage students to use the line plots to predict answers to some of the following questions. Suggest that they then test their predictions using the equal-arm balance.

   ■ How much more does a cupful of split peas weigh than a cupful of macaroni?

   ■ How much do four cupfuls of sunflower seeds weigh?

   ■ How much less does one cupful of sunflower seeds weigh than one cupful of split peas?

   ■ Which weighs more, three cupfuls of oat cereal or one cupful of macaroni?

   ■ Which weighs less, five cupfuls of oat cereal or two cupfuls of sunflower seeds?

MATHEMATICS

2. Have students use the information on the line plots to make a bar graph that shows the weights of a cupful of each of the four foods.

SCIENCE

3. Attach a strip of masking tape to several unlabeled cans of food. Then ask students to weigh each can with Unifix Cubes™ and write the weight on the tape. Then give students labeled cans whose contents are identical to those of the unlabeled ones. Ask students to predict what the unlabeled cans contain. Then have them weigh the labeled cans to solve this problem.

MATHEMATICS

4. Collect various foods or miscellaneous items to use in a classroom store. Challenge students to devise a monetary system and buy and sell items on the basis of weight.

Record Sheet 14-A

Name: --------------------------------

Date: --------------------------------

Weighing Cupfuls of Food

Food	Weight
Split peas	_____ cubes
Macaroni	_____ cubes
Sunflower seeds	_____ cubes
Oat cereal	_____ cubes

Which Food Occupies the Most Space?

Overview and Objectives

In the last lesson, students discovered that equal cupfuls of different foods have different weights. In this lesson, they will determine that equal weights of the four foods occupy different amounts of space. To make this discovery, they are challenged to reverse the weighing process. Instead of determining how many Unifix Cubes™ are needed to balance a certain amount of food, they will determine how much food is needed to balance a certain number of cubes.

- Students measure out equal weights of the four foods.

- Students observe which of the four foods occupies the most space.

- Students explain the reasons for their observations.

Background

In Lessons 13 and 14, students kept the size of the cup constant and observed that the weight of each cupful of food was different. In this lesson, they keep the weight of the foods constant and observe that each food takes up a different amount of space. The oat cereal, for example, will occupy almost twice as much space as any of the other foods. Figure 15-1 shows approximately how much space each food occupies in the cup.

Figure 15-1

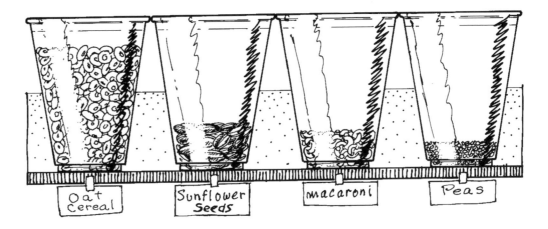

To complete the activities in this lesson, students will use a new weighing strategy. They will no longer put an object in one pail and add Unifix Cubes™ to the other pail until the equal-arm balance is level. Instead, they will start with a fixed number of Unifix Cubes™ and add food until the equal-arm balance is level. Some students may find this reversal confusing at first. They may need guidance at the beginning of the lesson to help them become comfortable with this new method of weighing.

Materials

For every two students

    1 equal-arm balance
    1 piece of clay
    10 Unifix Cubes™
    2 large plastic cups, 296 ml (10 oz)
    1 small plastic cup, 74 ml (2½ oz)

For the class

    2 plastic pails of round oat cereal, 340 g (12 oz)
    1 plastic pail of macaroni, 680 g (1½ lb)
    1 plastic pail of sunflower seeds, 450 g (1 lb)
    1 plastic pail of split peas, 1.3 kg (2½ lb)
    3 empty plastic pails
    4 line plots (from Lesson 14)
       "Describing the Foods" chart (from Lesson 12)
       "Why Cupfuls of Food Are Heavier and Lighter" chart (from Lesson 13)

Preparation

1. Each pair of students will weigh only two foods. Arrange for eight pairs of students to weigh macaroni and split peas and the remaining pairs to weigh sunflower seeds and oat cereal. Once they have weighed two foods, each pair will team with a pair of students that has weighed the other two foods and discuss their findings.

2. Students will be collecting foods and returning unused foods throughout this lesson. To avoid congestion, it is best to set up four food distribution centers, one for each food. Place the two pails of round oat cereal at one station. Divide the contents of the pails of peas, macaroni, and sunflower seeds in half, placing the food you have removed in the three extra pails. Put two pails of each food at the other three food centers. Place the remaining supplies in the regular distribution center.

3. Make sure that the two charts, "Describing the Foods" and "Why Cupfuls of Food Are Lighter and Heavier," as well as the four line plots, are on display.

Procedure

1. Ask students to review the line plots and then to think about how much of each food would weigh 10 Unifix Cubes™. Have them share their ideas.

2. Let students know that their challenge today will be to find out how much of each of the foods has the same weight as 10 Unifix Cubes™. Tell each pair of students which two foods they will be weighing. Inform them that after weighing their foods, they will team up with a pair of students who have weighed the other two foods and share their results.

3. Direct the students' attention to the four food centers. Let them know that each pair will work with only one food at a time. They will begin by collecting one small cupful of one food. If they need more, they will return to the food center to get it. When they have finished weighing the first food, they should return any unused food to the food center. They will repeat this process for the second food.

4. Have students collect the materials from the distribution center. After they have equilibrated the balances, have them pick up their foods and begin to weigh them.

Figure 15-2

Weighing a food with 10 Unifix Cubes™

5. Once they have weighed the first food, have students remove the pail from the S-hook and pour the food into the large plastic cup. Remind them to return any unused food to the appropriate food center. Then have them repeat the same procedure with the second food.

6. When all pairs of students have finished, have them return the equal-arm balances and Unifix Cubes™ to the distribution center.

Final Activities

1. Group the students in teams of four so that each team has one set of all four foods.

2. Ask the teams to place their four cups of food in serial order, left to right, beginning with the food that occupies the least space in the cup.

3. Direct students' attention to the charts entitled "Describing the Foods" and "Why Cupfuls of Food Are Heavier and Lighter" and the four line plots. Encourage students to use them and the observations they have just made to discuss the following questions:

■ Which food occupies the most space? The least space?

- How does this new serial order compare with that found in Lessons 13 and 14?

- Is the food that occupies the most space the heaviest or the lightest food?

- Is the food that occupies the least space the heaviest or the lightest food?

- Why is the cup of the smallest and heaviest food the least full?

- Why is the cup of the largest and lightest food the most full?

4. To help students summarize the discoveries they have made in the last three lessons, discuss the following questions:

- Why did the equal cupfuls of food weigh different amounts?

- Why did the foods take up different amounts of space, even though they all weighed the same?

5. Have students return all of the materials in the distribution center and replace the food in the containers.

Extensions

| MATHEMATICS | | SCIENCE |

1. Have students bring in boxes of various foods and find the weight printed on each box. Ask them to weigh each box with Unifix Cubes™ and create a data table to show how many Unifix Cubes™ equal the unit of weight printed on the box. Then ask students to consider these questions:

- Why would two packages that weigh the same be different sizes?

- What could you predict about the contents of each package on the basis of the weight and size of the package?

| SOCIAL STUDIES |

2. Have students find information on how manufacturers package foods. Invite a representative of a local manufacturer to visit the class and describe the process the company uses, or arrange a field trip to the company. Afterwards, have the students write and draw about what they learned. Then bind the pages into a class book.

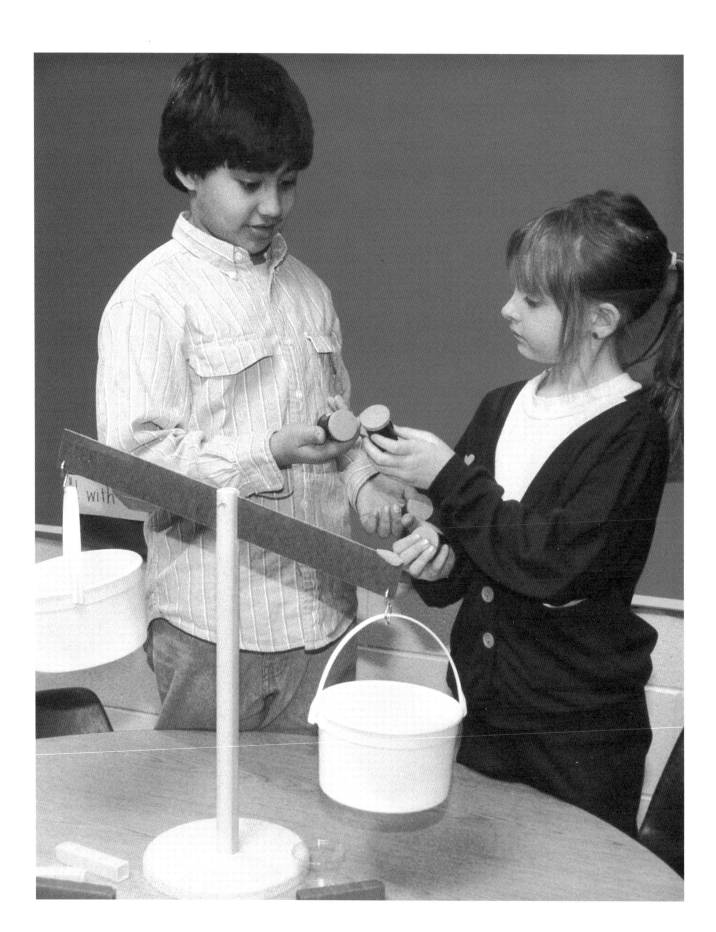

Where Are the Six Marbles?

Overview and Objectives

Which canister has six marbles? In this culminating lesson, students apply the skills and problem-solving strategies they have developed with the equal-arm balance to determine which of five sealed canisters contains six marbles. This activity is an embedded assessment that provides students with an opportunity to demonstrate what they have learned about comparing and weighing.

■ Students apply a strategy to discover which of five sealed canisters contains six marbles.

■ Students discuss the importance of the weight of the empty canister in solving this problem.

Background

Your students will probably approach the challenge that Lesson 16 poses in a number of ways. For example, they may

■ Weigh each canister using the Unifix Cubes™.

■ Use the equal-arm balance to compare each canister with the six marbles to find the one that weighs the same as the marbles.

■ Use the equal-arm balance to compare the canisters and place them in serial order.

■ Weigh each canister and weigh the six marbles and conclude that the canister that weighs the same as the six marbles is the one that contains six marbles.

All these strategies may be effective for solving some problems. The approaches do not, however, provide all the information that students will need to solve this problem, because they do not take into account the weight of the empty canister.

To determine which canister contains six marbles, students will need to find a way to include the weight of the canister in their calculations. Many students may have a sense that this additional weight should be taken into consideration, and they will probably explore various ways of doing so.

Nonetheless, figuring out how to account for the weight of the canister will be a challenge. After their initial explorations and a class discussion, students will probably need to return to the activity and apply other strategies that will account for the weight of the canister.

Materials

For every two students

  6 marbles
  1 equal-arm balance
  1 piece of clay
 20 Unifix Cubes™
  1 small plastic cup, 74 ml (2½ oz) (optional)
  2 sheets of writing paper

For the class

300 marbles
 75 film canisters with lids
 15 blue stickers
 15 red stickers
 15 green stickers
 15 yellow stickers
 15 orange stickers
  1 sheet of newsprint
  2 copies of the blackline master **The Canisters**
  5 colored markers (one each of red, blue, green, yellow, and orange)
     Transparent tape
     Magnets (optional)

Note: The marbles used in this lesson must be identical in weight. They must also be small enough so that as many as eight of them will fit into a film canister. If you make substitutions, be sure that the marbles you have selected meet both of these requirements.

Preparation

1. Prepare a set of five canisters for each pair of students. Figure 16-1 shows how many marbles to place in each canister and which colored sticker to attach to the side.

Management Tip: You may want to place a piece of transparent tape across each colored sticker to keep it from peeling off.

Figure 16-1

Number of Marbles in Each Canister

Canister Color	Number of Marbles
Orange	0
Green	2
Red	4
Blue	6
Yellow	8

2. Make two copies of the blackline master **The Canisters** (pg. 145). You will need five canisters. With the markers, color the circle on each canister to match the colored stickers on the students' canisters. Since you will later adhere these cutouts to a class data table, you may want to laminate them or cover them with transparent Con-Tact™ paper.

3. Display the sheet of newsprint in a visible area. You will use it to create a class data table in Step 1 of the **Final Activities.**

4. Arrange the materials in the distribution center. Place six marbles in each of the 15 small plastic cups, or use any other container that keeps the marbles from rolling. Place the canisters that you have labeled and filled with marbles in groups on the table. You may separate the canisters into five groups on the basis of color and have students collect one canister from each cluster. You could also arrange the canisters in sets of the five colors and ask students to collect one complete set.

Preparation

1. Show students the five film canisters and six marbles. Let them know that each canister contains a different number of marbles.

2. Ask pairs of students to discuss how they could find out which canister has six marbles. After a few minutes, have students share their ideas with the class. Let them know they will now try some of the strategies they have just discussed.

3. Ask students to collect the materials from the distribution center. Have them equilibrate their equal-arm balances and then begin the activity.

4. Encourage students to record what they discover about the canisters on the writing paper as they conduct the activity.

Figure 16-2

Comparing the canisters

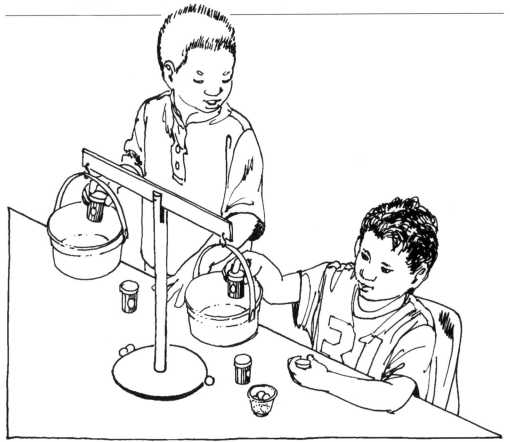

5. If students need additional guidance, ask some of the following questions:

- What could you find out about the six marbles that would give you information to help you solve the problem?

- How could you compare the canisters to find the one that has six marbles?

- How could you use the Unifix Cubes™ to find the canister that has six marbles?

6. After students have decided which canister they think holds the six marbles, ask them to write the color of that canister's sticker on a sheet of writing paper.

7. Have students keep their materials at their desks, since they will probably want to continue their explorations after the class discussion. Ask them to move the materials to the side of their desks during the discussion.

Final Activities

1. Record what students discovered about the canisters on the data table. Create the columns for this table as students share information with you. For example, some students may have placed the canisters in serial order. You can show this by placing your cutouts in that order in a column along the left side of the data table. If some students weighed the canisters, you can create a column to record the weights. Figure 16-3 illustrates an example of the information that could be included on the data table.

2. Ask students to share which canister they think has the six marbles. Ask them to describe the reasons for their decisions. What did they learn about the canisters and the marbles that led them to conclude that a specific canister contains the six marbles?

3. Ask students to discuss how the weight of the canister affected both their strategies and their results.

4. The rest of this lesson will depend on the results of students' initial explorations. If some students simply placed the canisters in serial order, they may want to weigh them now. If some students selected a canister with fewer than six marbles because they had not developed a strategy that accounted for the weight of the canister, they may also want to resume their investigations. After students have completed a second round of explorations, you will want to have them regroup for further discussion.

Extensions

SCIENCE

1. After students find the canister with six marbles, challenge them to solve other problems.

- Do any of the canisters have more than six marbles?

- Which canisters have fewer than six marbles?

- How could you find out how many marbles are in each canister?

SCIENCE

2. Create another "hidden weight" activity by using empty milk cartons, margarine tubs, or other containers. For example, fill six small milk cartons with different amounts of sand and two additional cartons with equal amounts of sand. Label each carton with a sticker. Ask students to pick

Figure 16-3

Sample data table

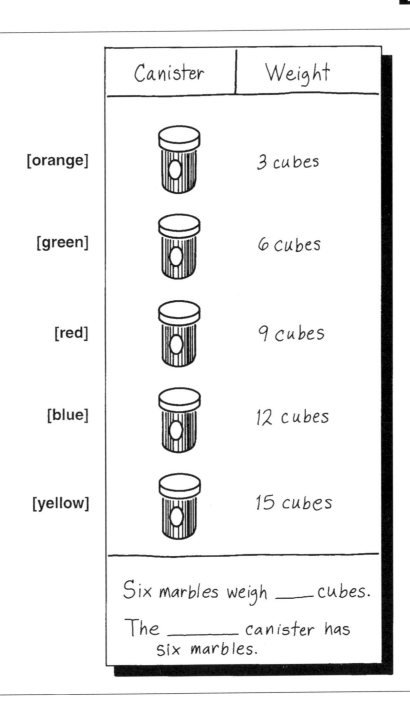

Canister	Weight
[orange]	3 cubes
[green]	6 cubes
[red]	9 cubes
[blue]	12 cubes
[yellow]	15 cubes

Six marbles weigh ____cubes.

The _____ canister has six marbles.

them up and answer the following questions. After students have answered the questions, have them use the equal-arm balance to weigh the cartons.

■ Which carton is the heaviest?

■ Which carton is the lightest?

■ Can you place all eight cartons in serial order from lightest to heaviest?

■ Can you find two cartons that weigh the same amount?

Assessment   Lesson 16 is an embedded assessment that challenges students to apply much of what they have learned during the unit. To assess students' progress, observe the following areas:

- Which strategy do students apply to solve the problem?

- How do students account for the weight of the canister?

- What conclusions do students draw from their results?

- What reasons do students use to support their conclusions?

Post-Unit Assessment

The post-unit assessment (pgs. 147–148) is a matched follow-up to the pre-unit assessment in Lesson 1. Comparing students' pre- and post-unit responses to the same set of questions allows you to document their learning.

Additional Assessments

Additional assessments for this unit are on pgs. 149–153.

The Canisters

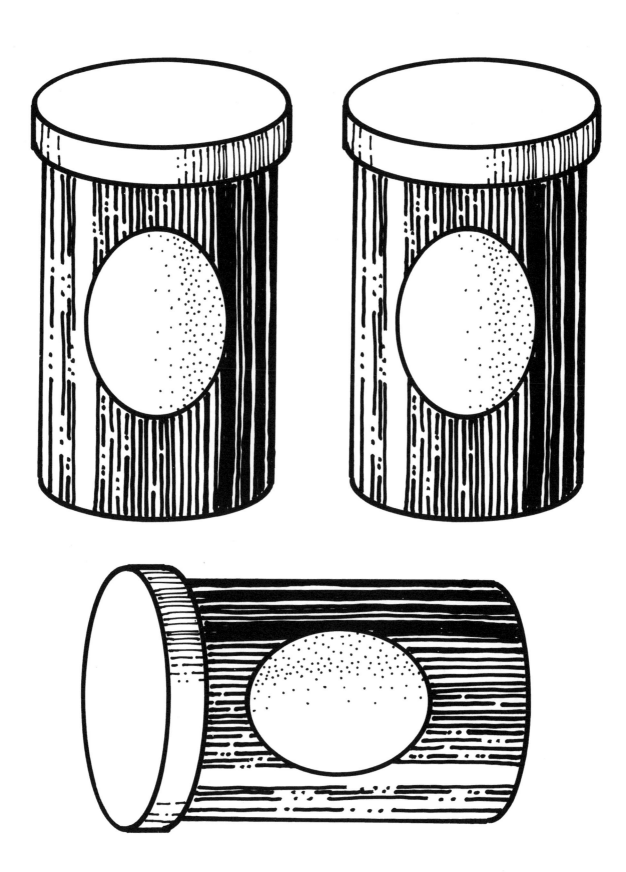

Post-Unit Assessment

Overview

This activity is the second part of the matched pre- and post-unit assessment. During the brainstorming session in Lesson 1, the class developed two lists— "What We Know about Balancing" and "What We Would Like to Know about Balancing." When students revisit these questions during the post-unit assessment, you will have an opportunity to evaluate what they have learned about balancing. The post-unit assessment does not include comparing and weighing; however, the activities in Lesson 16 are an embedded assessment of students' knowledge of comparing and weighing. The additional assessments (pgs. 149–153) provide suggestions for activities that you may use to assess what your students have learned about comparing and weighing.

Materials

For each student
   1   science journal

For the class
   1   sheet of newsprint
   1   marker
       "What We Know about Balancing" and "What We Would Like to Know about Balancing" charts (from Lesson 1)

Preparation

1. On the sheet of newsprint, write the title "What We Know about Balancing" and the current date.

2. Have the class charts from Lesson 1 ready, but do not post them until Step 3 of the **Procedure.**

Procedure

1. Distribute the science journals and ask students to write their ideas in response to the statement "What I know about balancing." After a few minutes, ask students to write the questions they have about balancing.

2. Invite students to share some of the ideas they wrote in response to the first question. Record these on the new chart, "What We Know about Balancing."

3. Display the charts from Lesson 1. First, ask students to compare the comments on the two "What We Know about Balancing" charts. Ask them to look at the list from Lesson 1 and tell you if it contains any statements that

they now know are incorrect. Then ask them to discuss any comments on the new list that do not appear on the list from Lesson 1. This comparison will help students recognize how much they have learned.

4. Now ask students to look at the other chart from Lesson 1, "What We Would Like to Know about Balancing." Have them identify any questions that they have now answered. Invite them to add new questions from their journal entries in this lesson and to suggest how they might answer them.

5. After the lesson, collect students' science journals and compare their responses to questions in the post-unit assessment with those from Lesson 1. As you compare the entries, look for the following:

   ■ What activities from the unit are contained in students' post-unit responses? For example, do students describe their experiences with the butterfly, mobile, beam balance, and equal-arm balance?

   ■ In what ways do students' post-unit responses show more detail than those from Lesson 1? Do the students provide more elaborate descriptions of balancing?

   ■ In what ways do students show growth in their ability to express themselves through drawings and writing?

Additional Assessments

Overview

This section presents four suggested assessment activities. Although not essential, they can provide additional information that will help you evaluate student learning. Consider using various kinds of assessments so that students with different learning styles will have opportunities to express their knowledge and skills.

- **Assessment 1** asks students to write in their science journals in response to the question "What have you learned about balancing and weighing?"

- **Assessment 2** is a follow-up to Lesson 4, in which students explored how the position of the fulcrum affects balance.

- **Assessment 3** is a review of the record sheets, writing, drawings, and graphs that students have produced throughout the unit. It also suggests guidelines for conducting student conferences.

- **Assessment 4** describes hands-on activities that you may use to assess students' growth.

Assessment 1: Writing about Balancing and Weighing

Students write in their science journals in response to the question "What have you learned about balancing and weighing?" Teachers have found that this open-ended question often elicits reflective writing by children.

Materials

For each student
- 1 science journal
- 1 pencil

Procedure

1. Distribute the science journals. Ask students to write in response to the question "What have you learned about balancing and weighing?"

2. As you review the science journals, look for evidence of growth in students' knowledge. Watch specifically for descriptions that reflect an understanding that the amount of weight, position of weight, and position of the fulcrum affect balance. Note instances where students support their descriptions with examples of activities from the unit, such as balancing the butterfly, making a mobile, placing objects or cupfuls of food in serial order, and comparing and weighing. Also look for evidence that students are aware of how balancing and

weighing are used in the world around them, such as discussions about Calder's mobiles, weighing animals at the zoo, or gymnastics.

Assessment 2: Fulcrum Position

Building on their experiences in Lesson 4, students predict where to place the fulcrum under a beam that holds unevenly distributed numbers of Unifix Cubes™. They make predictions about where the beam will balance, slide the beam across the fulcrum to test their predictions, and record their results.

Materials

For each student
1   copy of **Record Sheet A-1: Fulcrum Position**
1   completed copy of **Record Sheet 4-A: Where Is the Fulcrum?** (from Lesson 4)

For every two students
1   fulcrum
1   beam
20   Unifix Cubes™

Preparation

1. Make one copy of **Record Sheet A-1: Fulcrum Position** (pg. 153) for each student.

2. Have students' copies of completed **Record Sheet 4-A: Where Is the Fulcrum?** ready to distribute in Step 4 of the **Procedure.**

3. Arrange the beams, fulcrums, and Unifix Cubes™ in the distribution center.

Procedure

1. Remind students that in Lesson 4 they explored how moving the fulcrum affected how the beam balanced. Let them know that they will now complete a similar activity using different arrangements of Unifix Cubes™.

2. Distribute one copy of **Record Sheet A-1: Fulcrum Position** to each student. Ask students to draw the fulcrum under each beam to show where they predict it should be in order to make the beam balance.

3. Have pairs of students collect the materials and test their predictions. Remind them to write their results on the record sheets.

4. Distribute students' completed copies of **Record Sheet 4A: Where Is the Fulcrum?** Ask them to compare and discuss Record Sheets 4-A and A-1. Ask them to describe what they know now that helped them predict where to place the fulcrum.

5. To help you assess students' growth, listen for some of the following ideas as they describe their results:

   ■ If the weight on each end of the beam is equal, the fulcrum must be in the middle.

   ■ If there is more weight on one end of the beam than on the other, the fulcrum has to be moved closer to the greater weight.

   ■ The position of the Unifix Cubes™ affects how the beam balances.

6. Throughout this activity, assess how well students apply what they learned from their experiences with the beam balance to help them describe the various positions of the fulcrum, beam, and Unifix Cubes™.

Assessment 3: Student Work and Individual Conferences

Reviewing each student's work products can help you assess his or her growth during the unit. In this assessment, you will evaluate students' record sheets, graphs, science journal entries, and drawings. If you combine such a review with conferences during which individual students or student pairs share with you what they have learned, you will have an even more comprehensive view of each student's growth.

Materials

Collection of individual work products: record sheets, graphs, serial order strips, science journals, drawings, and any other products created during the unit

Procedure

1. Assemble each student's work products. As you review the products, consider the following:

   ■ How complete are the products?

   ■ Do the products (especially the graph and serial order strip) indicate effort on the student's part?

   ■ Which activities were hardest for the student to do? Which concepts were most difficult to grasp?

   ■ Do the products reflect a growth in the student's knowledge, skills, and understanding?

3. Meet with students individually or in pairs. During these conferences, you may want to have students respond to the following:

   ■ Describe how moving the fulcrum affects the way the beam balances.

   ■ How are the beam balance and equal-arm balance alike? How are they different? How is a mobile like a beam balance? An equal-arm balance?

   ■ Describe how you know that weight affects balance.

   ■ Describe how you would compare two objects to see which is heavier. How would you know if the objects weighed the same?

   ■ How would you define weighing?

   ■ Are big objects always heavy? How do you know this?

   ■ What are some of the factors that determine how much a cupful of food weighs?

   ■ In this unit, you recorded information on data tables, bar graphs, and line plots. Which was the most helpful way to present information? Why?

Assessment 4: Hands-On Activities

One valuable way to assess students' progress is to ask them to apply their skills to solve new problems. In this way, students are expressing their knowledge in the manner in which they learned it—through hands-on activities. Listed below are ideas for activities that challenge students to solve a problem using skills they acquired in this unit.

One way to administer this assessment is to arrange the activities in a "circus" format. To arrange the circus, place the materials needed for each activity in a separate center. Have students rotate among the centers.

To assess students' growth, evaluate the strategies they use, the methods they apply, the way they record their results, and their explanations for their solutions to problems. Finding the "right" answer is less important than applying an effective strategy and supporting their explanations with solid reasons based on observation and experience.

- Use the equal-arm balance to find out which weighs more, a wet sponge or a dry sponge.

- Use the equal-arm balance to find out which weighs more, equal cupfuls of popcorn kernels or popped popcorn.

- Use miscellaneous materials, such as cork, wire, wood beads, pieces of sponge, or Styrofoam™ balls, to create a balance toy.

- Weigh miscellaneous objects and create a data table or bar graph to show their weights.

Name: -

Date: -

Fulcrum Position

Draw the fulcrum to show how the beam balanced.

Bibliography: Resources for Teachers and Books for Students

The Bibliography is divided into the following categories:

- Resources for Teachers
- Books for Students

While not a complete list of books written about balancing and weighing, this bibliography is a sampling of books that complement the unit. The materials come well recommended. They have been favorably reviewed, and teachers have found them useful.

If a book goes out of print or if you seek additional titles, you may wish to consult the following resources.

Appraisal: Science Books for Young People (The Children's Science Book Review Committee, Boston).

Published quarterly, this periodical reviews new science books available for young people. Each book is reviewed by a librarian and a scientist. The Children's Science Book Review Committee is sponsored by the Science Education Department of Boston University's School of Education and the New England Roundtable of Children's Librarians.

National Science Resources Center. *Science for Children: Resources for Teachers.* Washington, DC: National Academy Press, 1988.

This volume provides a wealth of information about resources for hands-on science programs. It describes science curriculum materials, supplementary materials (science activity books, books on teaching science, reference books, and magazines), museum programs, and elementary science curriculum projects.

Science and Children (National Science Teachers Association, Arlington, VA).

Each March, this monthly periodical provides an annotated bibliography of outstanding children's science trade books primarily for pre-kindergarten through eighth-grade science teachers.

Science Books & Films (American Association for the Advancement of Science, Washington, DC).

Published nine times a year, this periodical offers critical reviews of a wide range of new science materials, from books to audiovisual materials to electronic resources. The reviews are written primarily by scientists and science educators. *Science Books & Films* is useful for librarians, media specialists, curriculum supervisors, science teachers, and others responsible for recommending and purchasing scientific materials.

Scientific American (Scientific American, Inc., New York).

Each December, Philip and Phylis Morrison compile and review a selection of outstanding new science books for children.

Sosa, Maria, and Shirley Malcom, eds. *Science Books & Films: Best Books for Children, 1988–91.* Washington, DC: American Association for the Advancement of Science Press, 1992.

This volume, part of a continuing series, is a compilation of the most highly rated science books that have been reviewed recently in the periodical *Science Books & Films.*

Resources for Teachers

Charlesworth, Rosalind, and Karen K. Lind. *Math and Science for Young Children.* New York: Delmar Publishers, Inc., 1990.

This well-written book is designed to be used by teachers wishing to teach math and science on the basis of a developmental sequence of learning. Activities are suggested for presenting numerous math and science skills, topics, and concepts. The authors also provide a "developmentally appropriate assessment" that matches the sequence of skills students are challenged to master. Skills and concepts suggested in this book can be used to supplement those taught in the *Balancing and Weighing* unit.

Dishon, Dee, and Pat Wilson O'Leary. *A Guidebook for Cooperative Learning: Techniques for Creating More Effective Schools.* Holmes Beach, FL: Learning Publications, Inc., 1984.

This practical guide helps teachers implement cooperative-learning techniques in the classroom.

Johnson, David W., Roger T. Johnson, and Edythe Johnson Holubec. *Circles of Learning: Cooperation in the Classroom.* Alexandria, VA: Association for Supervision and Curriculum Development, 1984.

This book presents the case for cooperative learning in a concise, readable form. It reviews the research, outlines implementation strategies, and answers many questions.

Labinowicz, Ed. *The Piaget Primer: Thinking-Learning-Teaching.* Illustrated by Susie Pollard Frazee. Menlo Park, CA: Addison-Wesley Publishing Company, 1980.

Suitable for both the novice and expert, this is a detailed but readable text about child growth and development. The author uses practical examples to illustrate his ideas. The book contains an in-depth analysis of the developmental concepts that are included in the *Balancing and Weighing* unit.

Lipman, Jean. *Calder's Universe.* New York: Harrison House, 1980.

This large and colorful book contains beautiful illustrations and photographs of Alexander Calder's art as well as a biography of the artist. Lipman, who was a friend of Calder, has written numerous books about him.

Books for Students

Evans, David, and Claudette Williams. *Make It Balance.* New York: Dorling Kindersley, Inc., 1992.

This book is geared toward young children. The photographs are bold and descriptive, and the text is age-appropriate. An introductory note to parents and teachers describes the importance of student exploration with safe and interesting materials. Students can use this book independently in a learning center or for take-home activities.

Fitzpatrick, Julie. *Balancing.* Illustrated by Diana Bowles. Englewood Cliffs, NJ: Silver Burdett Press, 1988.

This book contains activities that are designed to encourage students to explore balance. It contains illustrations and clear directions for making balance toys and mobiles and creating balances with fulcrums. The text defines terms such as balance, lever, fulcrum, balance point, and mass in simple words.

Jennings, Terry. *Balancing.* Illustrated by David Anstey. New York: Gloucester Press, 1989.

This book contains illustrations that show children involved in balancing activities: playing on seesaws, walking on beams, and riding tricycles and bicycles. It also provides simple directions for making balance toys and mobiles.

Lipman, Jean, and Margaret Aspinwall. *Alexander Calder and His Magical Mobiles.* New York: Hudson Hills Press, Inc., 1981.

Although written for older children, this book is appropriate for reading to younger children. The authors describe Calder's life and the various styles of art he created, from animal sketches to mobiles. The book is illustrated with color and black-and-white photographs of Calder's works. The bibliography contains a list of places across the United States where Calder's mobiles are on display. This book is a suitable complement to Lesson 5 of the *Balancing and Weighing* unit.

McCully, Emily Arnold. *Mirette on the High Wire.* New York: The Putnam Publishing Group, 1992.

Emily McCully's watercolor illustrations enhance her story about a little girl's friendship with a tightrope walker who has become afraid of walking the high wire. Mirette learns to walk the rope and, in the process, helps "The Great Bellini" rebuild his courage. This book complements the reading selection in Lesson 3 of the *Balancing and Weighing* unit.

National Science Resources Center Advisory Board

Chair

Joseph A. Miller, Jr., Chief Technology Officer and Senior Vice President for Research and Development, DuPont Company, Wilmington, Del.

Members

Ann Bay, Director, Office of Education, Smithsonian Institution, Washington, D.C.

DeAnna Banks Beane, Project Director, YouthALIVE, Association of Science-Technology Centers, Washington, D.C.

Fred P. Corson, Vice President and Director, Research and Development, The Dow Chemical Company, Midland, Mich.

Goéry Delacôte, Executive Director, The Exploratorium, San Francisco, Calif.

JoAnn E. DeMaria, Teacher, Hutchison Elementary School, Herndon, Va.

Peter Dow, Director of Education, Buffalo Museum of Science, Buffalo, N.Y.

Hubert M. Dyasi, Director, The Workshop Center, City College School of Education (The City University of New York), New York, N.Y.

Bernard S. Finn, Curator, Division of Information Technology and Society, National Museum of American History, Smithsonian Institution, Washington, D.C.

Robert M. Fitch, President, Fitch & Associates, Taos, N.M.

Jerry P. Gollub, John and Barbara Bush Professor in the Natural Sciences, Haverford College, Haverford, Pa.

Ana M. Guzmán, Vice President, Cypress Creek Campus and Institutional Campus Development, Austin Community College, Austin, Tex.

Anders Hedberg, Director, Center for Science Education, Bristol-Myers Squibb Pharmaceutical Research Institute, Princeton, N.J.

Richard Hinman, Senior Vice President (retired), Central Research Division, Pfizer Inc., Groton, Conn.

David Jenkins, Associate Director for Interpretive Programs, National Zoological Park, Smithsonian Institution, Washington, D.C.

Mildred E. Jones, Educational Consultant, Baldwin, N.Y.

John W. Layman, Director, Science Teaching Center, and Professor, Departments of Education and Physics, University of Maryland, College Park, Md.

Leon M. Lederman, Chair, Board of Trustees, Teachers Academy for Mathematics and Science, Chicago, Ill., and Director Emeritus, Fermi National Accelerator Laboratory, Batavia, Ill.

Sarah A. Lindsey, Science Coordinator, Midland Public Schools, Midland, Mich.

Lynn Margulis, Distinguished University Professor, Department of Botany, University of Massachusetts, Amherst, Mass.

Ted A. Maxwell, Associate Director, Collections and Research, National Air and Space Museum, Smithsonian Institution, Washington, D.C.

Mara Mayor, Director, The Smithsonian Associates, Smithsonian Institution, Washington, D.C.

John A. Moore, Professor Emeritus, Department of Biology, University of California, Riverside, Calif.

Carlo Parravano, Director, Merck Institute for Science Education, Rahway, N.J.

Robert W. Ridky, Program Director, Division of Undergraduate Education/Geosciences, National Science Foundation, Arlington, Va.

Ruth O. Selig, Executive Officer for Programs, Office of the Provost, Smithsonian Institution, Washington, D.C.

Maxine F. Singer, President, Carnegie Institution of Washington, Washington, D.C.

Robert D. Sullivan, Associate Director for Public Programs, National Museum of Natural History, Smithsonian Institution, Washington, D.C.

Gerald F. Wheeler, Executive Director, National Science Teachers Association, Arlington, Va.

Richard L. White, Executive Vice President, Bayer Corporation, Pittsburgh, Pa., and President of Fibers, Organics, and Rubber Division, and President and Chief Executive Officer, Bayer Rubber Inc., Canada

Paul H. Williams, Atwood Professor, Department of Plant Pathology, University of Wisconsin, Madison, Wis.

Karen L. Worth, Faculty, Wheelock College, and Senior Associate, Urban Elementary Science Project, Education Development Center, Newton, Mass.

Ex Officio Members

Rodger Bybee, Executive Director, Center for Science, Mathematics, and Engineering Education, National Research Council, Washington, D.C.

E. William Colglazier, Executive Officer, National Academy of Sciences, Washington, D.C.

J. Dennis O'Connor, Provost, Smithsonian Institution, Washington, D.C.

Barbara Schneider, Executive Assistant for Programs, Office of the Provost, Smithsonian Institution, Washington, D.C.

DATE DUE

FEB 1 8 2000			
7/6/02			
2/26/04			
MAR 3 1 2006			
GAYLORD			PRINTED IN U.S.A.